# Survival in Society

# Survival in Society

**Eugene Heimler**

**Weidenfeld and Nicolson**
London

Weidenfeld and Nicolson
11 St John's Hill
London SW11

ISBN 0 297 76841 7
Printed and bound in Great Britain by
by Redwood Burn Limited Trowbridge & Esher

# Contents

# Introduction

When I put myself in another's hands, it is I who have decided and who go on deciding he will direct me; thus I do not transfer the decision itself, but merely its mechanism.

*Socrates*

As they grow up, most people learn how to manage the many and various problems that confront them; they learn how to lead comparatively positive lives, how to find satisfactions that make life worth while, and how to turn frustrations and difficulties into useful potential driving forces. Often one part of their lives, either at work or at home, in the family or in a leisure activity, more than compensates for any difficulties they find elsewhere: it is often the immense pleasure gained from doing what they enjoy that enables them to weather the storms. In fact, most people adapt quickly to new situations, are naturally spontaneous and creative and rather enjoy the challenges posed by changing circumstances.

From time to time we all experience great emotional stress, pain and misery. No one is free from problems and everyone wanders occasionally into a no-man's land between sanity and insanity. The human situation is such that not to be abnormal at times would be a true sign of abnormality. But we learn to integrate these moments into our personalities and use them to enrich our lives. We learn how to take positive action so that we keep going despite our setbacks. Indeed, sometimes we even learn to turn setbacks into positive advantages.

However, many people become unable to make use of their frustrations; they can no longer go about their daily lives and function in society because they have reached a crisis point at which their problems overwhelm them. So great are their frustrations, emotions and difficulties that they often feel quite unable to make decisions of any kind, or even to work or mix with other people. These people have many labels attached to them: they are mentally or emotionally 'disordered', workshy, unemployable, hysterical, depressed. But they all suffer from the same problem: the relationship of satisfaction and frustration in their lives is out of balance, and the frustrations so outweigh the pleasures that they are temporarily defeated. Moreover, they are unable to distance themselves sufficiently from their difficulties to see where the real tangle lies. As they cannot disentangle the crux of their problems from the general surrounding gloom, they cannot begin to take any positive action to help themselves.

It is my contention that some of these people *can* be helped, quickly and clearly, if a skilled trained person, an 'interviewer', applies techniques which I am going to describe.

The interviewer can help the patient disentangle his thoughts and get him to be clear and concise about his dilemma; he can get some perspective on the patient's worries and help him to see them for what they are. The problems are not always unanswerable or insuperable once they are laid bare: often they are the result of social conditioning or of circumstance. Once a person has seen his own problems psychologically externalized — written down on paper — and has been able to consider them objectively he can often solve them himself. The interviewer is not there to interfere and organize, to interpret or to answer, but to question. He does not know the answer: only the patient does. The interviewer's task is to create a framework in which the patient can be in touch with his own experiences. The patient becomes his own therapist, and out of his own knowledge and experience he learns to help himself even when he is away from the consulting-room.

The course the interviews take are dictated by the patient's situation, for each meeting must be spontaneous and creative: the drive and direction must come from the patient. The interviews do not therefore necessarily follow each other in the order suggested here, although very often they do so.

At the first interview the patient is sympathetically encouraged to discuss his life. At the second, a set of fifty-five specially chosen questions (the Heimler Scale of Social Functioning) will be asked, and at the third interview the individual will be requested to give a fifteen-minute résumé of some aspect of his life that occurred in the last twenty-four hours — 'a slice of life'. In the final session (though of course it may take longer, or even less long, to reach this stage) he will be asked to *imagine* someone or something wise and benevolent who can guide him with his problems. The result of this 'dialogue' will be written down by the patient in a concise form, or he can say it into a tape-recorder; he will then listen to it read out or played back to him. After discussion this statement is again summarized by the patient in an even terser form.

In this way the patient's problem is externalized so that he can objectively see or listen to himself giving his own statement about his own experience. The very act of hearing his own dilemma played back to him or read out aloud often provokes patients to think of positive actions they can take immediately to remedy their situation. Most leave their third or fourth session full of ideas for action.

Results are measured by actions taken, by different patterns of coping mechanisms. The interviewer puts an implicit trust in the patient's ability to choose positive rather than negative actions once his own choices, through his own endeavours, are made clear to him.

A painter thinks emotionally and intellectually of what he wishes to express in his painting, then learns to externalize his thoughts and create them outside himself on canvas. All people have this ability to externalize their feelings and act positively on them. This method of self-treatment encourages the release of that creative ability in people, so that those who have ceased to function can return to society as useful, positive, creative members.

At the moment many emotionally and mentally disturbed people either are left alone to manage as best they can or have expensive sessions of psychoanalysis or psychotherapy. These psychotherapeutic practices aim to find out *why* this person is worrying himself sick. While trying to find out the why, they hope the person will be cured and often he is. But I believe in putting the individual firmly in the centre of his own world by bestirring his own will and his ability to change his own situation so that he can get on with his life: this is just as important. I feel that people should be encouraged to assess all the facets of their lives — the good, bad and indifferent bits — and that they should then be urged to use what they have to help themselves. They should be positively encouraged to make the best of the areas of satisfaction that they already possess and to use their frustrations in a useful fashion to impel them along, with a minimum amount of interference.

It is not possible to cure or remove all the difficulties a person encounters at any given moment, but they can often be put in a more favourable light and be seen for what they are — not insuperable or impossible but just problems that can be dealt with. I do not offer a cure, but rather suggest that much suffering can be alleviated, and many unhappy people helped out of a dilemma so that they can again function in society, if they can only be made to integrate all their experiences and use them for their own benefit. For I believe that neurosis is not so much a psychological state as an inability to cope with the experiences of life.

This book attempts to show through case histories and examples how this process of self-discovery is accomplished; how I came to have my various ideas, how they work, what they are, the methods and techniques. At the moment there are a great many people training to use the method of social functioning in England, Canada, Germany, the United States and elsewhere. In these countries nearly two thousand people are already trained and at work applying this method. Some of them have been doing so since 1970. This book is therefore not a final draft of an old and tried technique, but rather an interim report on an idea which is pragmatically proven to work and which is only at the beginning of its usefulness.

I hope this book will give readers some insight into their own problems and moments of despair and help them to understand those around them who are at variance with themselves, and that they will also be interested in the underlying philosophy behind these concepts. Finally, I hope that it will encourage and assist all those who are already at work with the lonely, the distressed and those temporarily unable to function in society — especially people in the 'helping' professions such as teachers, clergymen, social workers, doctors and nurses — to see their roles somewhat differently.

# 1 The Development of the Method

My interest in the relationship of satisfaction and frustration as experienced by the individual and in his ability to
turn pain to good account began when I was placed in
Buchenwald, Auschwitz and other extermination camps as a
young man of twenty-two, during the Second World War.

At one of these camps the SS Commandant embarked on a
'mental health experiment' to establish the way in which
useless and purposeless work would attack the prisoners'
will to live, and to 'measure' how many of them *in fact*
would commit suicide. This 'experiment' proved to be highly
successful from the point of view of the SS. We had been
ordered to carry sand and rubble from one end of the com-
pound to the other, about four miles, and then to carry it
back again. Within a few days 'results' began to accrue.
Some of my companions, mainly middle-aged men, simply gave
up the ghost and died; others ran against the electrified
wire that surrounded the camp and committed suicide; and
many more escaped into 'internal immigration' and became
insane.

I too began to notice feelings within myself that were
alien to my past experience. I seemed to be floating along in
an endless dream, even in daytime. Within this dream I was
able to stand back and look at myself working away as though
I were someone else: the detached, dreaming me was relaxed
and happy and gazed at the exhausted, working me as though
projected on a film screen. During these times of extreme
detachment I used to think of my mother, of my childhood
and of all the pleasurable things that had happened to me
in the past, and this seemed to give me hope, so that when I
woke up from these trance-like periods I had the strength to
survive.

My own emotional survival, I believe, was due to two main
factors: first, that somehow I was able to draw on love
received in the past, and second, my belief that, in order
to be able to move towards the future, I had to do something

about my dangerous predicament. I made an attempt to escape from the concentration camp and when I did so, although I exposed myself to very grave risks of being killed, the ghosts of the inner world disappeared. Meaning and action, therefore, seem to have played an important part in maintaining my sanity and in my remaining alive.

When the war was over and I returned to a more normal and civilized existence I asked myself: 'on what does it depend, whether we are defeated by life or whether we succeed?'. It appeared that if one can turn destructive forces towards some form of construction and 'madness' towards health then one can redirect one's own internal psychic energy in an outward and positive direction. The important message was the relationship between past and present, particularly as these affect the future. It appeared that, whatever my past experience had been, provided I was capable of finding *some* satisfying 'niche' in the present, I could function in the 'here and now' and find alternative choices for my future. The satisfying niche in my own case, when all other human satisfactions were absent and the last purposeful activity was also taken away, was a movement inwards, or rather backwards, into the past, and I clung desperately to the love that I had received then. This love, coupled with hope, enabled me to act, and a combination of these two paved my way towards my personal and professional future.

Cruelty and kindness are both part of the human condition: human destruction existed and still exists on a huge scale in the modern world. Today Auschwitz and the concentration camps appear as part of a larger Auschwitz that has occurred in Vietnam, in Pakistan — in Belfast and in the Middle East. In all these places the same problems occur; people are fighting for survival in the midst of self-destruction and insanity, and a great many are indeed surviving with their minds intact.

Some people however do not have to have been in the midst of battle to become ill; some people carry their own Auschwitz around with them, a burden that is often unbearable. When some of these people have come to see me as patients they have often presented their past experiences in an entirely negative light; or else (like myself) they have seen the past as the only source of satisfaction in contrast to a devastating present. Yet as treatment proceeded and they began to be able to function in the present and to cope better with their lives and problems, the perception they had of their past often changed. Living a more satisfactory present, some presented a previously-declared devastating past in a much more positive way, and others, who had drawn entirely on a positive past, began to see that it was not so happy as they previously presented it.

In both instances present satisfactions and the ability to achieve more satisfying coping mechanisms led the way to a more balanced picture of past experiences. At first tentatively, and later on with somewhat greater clarity, I had to conclude that not only had the past influenced the present, but the satisfactions of the present had also influenced the way one perceived one's past.

More and more, human problems seem to boil down to the possibility of alternative choices. Such alternatives give my patients hope, and when actual coping with problems begins, faith or confidence often enables them to function on a long-term basis much better than before. It seems that human actions in the present that offer or give one satisfaction are also channels through which one can select different memories from the past. In this sense, therefore, these patients may free themselves from a negative influence of the past through their actions in the present, or alternatively they may be able to free themselves from regressive behaviour which belonged to another age. It is also possible that if one is denied, or is incapable of finding, satisfying expressions in the present, then the unexpressed, unfulfilled, unformulated fantasies of the past may have a destructive influence on one's present; or alternatively it may become the only source of satisfaction available. Man is not only what he is but what he does; and what he does alters what he is.

If I further reflect on my wartime memories, I see with somewhat greater clarity the importance of experience. I suppose that experience is living that adds to my knowing, and knowledge consist of that which I observe (which is an intellectual activity) and that which I feel. Very often, however, during the process of living we have difficulties in integrating our observations with our feelings.

Although we go through millions of experiences every day, we are more often than not unable to perceive or make meaning of these experiences. Life can appear as a series of unconnected and meaningless 'happenings'; moments of joy and sadness can be considered as fragments of coincidences without any significance. If we cannot step outside and look at what is going on in our lives, we may easily become mere objects, whose destiny is in the hands of others. This alienation of thought and feeling may lead to a dullness of human experience, and at the same time to alienation from others.

My work with the unemployed in London, after I qualified as a psychiatric social worker, was one of my attempts to educe answers to questions I had formulated after the war. What happens to men and women if purposeful activity is not possible? In order to work some of these great puzzles and anxieties out of my system I tried to see whether I could be of any assistance to people who for *any* reason had been unemployed for a very long time. After all, I felt, the nightmare of purposeless activity in Auschwitz and the subsequent destruction and damage to thousands of people might have some relevance to the unemployed of this country.

The details of this work have been reported elsewhere.* Briefly, about 50 per cent of the unemployed returned to long-term employment within six months to a year. The question was then why complete failure had occurred in the other half of my caseload. The search for that answer was neither easy nor quick. It took me many years and many mistakes before I saw a pattern evolving which began to make some sense. Through follow-up studies undertaken over five years, it appeared that those who 'functioned' in society, as against those who did not 'function', had the common feature of a subjectively felt satisfaction that corresponded with their level of bearable frustration. This factor did not give the reasons for these people's original problems (or still-existing ones), but it did at least state some facts about them. What was important and relevant to me, however, was

* Eugene Heimler, *Mental Illness and Social Work* (London 1969), pp. 107-299.

that, for those who did function, more often than not subjective experiences of the self were closely linked with objective reality. For example, when someone reported feeling more satisfied about his financial situation, the actual management of such finances as well as income level was more satisfactory not only to the individual concerned but to those closely involved in his life. And at the other end of the scale, for example, those who had reported difficulties in inter-personal relationships *did* have problems in this area, which were reported by others involved in their environment.

Subjectivity and objectivity, it appeared, were interwoven to a point at which one began to wonder whether the two could be separated. After all, in philosophical terms, what is absolute reality? It appeared that society, or the 'outer world', was not always the best judge when evaluating the sense of wellbeing that some individuals or groups of individuals had experienced.

It was possible, for example, for two damaged individuals, a man and a woman, to fit their damage (subjectively felt by themselves and, say, objectively observed by doctors) in such a way that they could make a satisfying relationship with each other. In the extreme I have come across a number of cases where such satisfactions in marital relationships depended on mutual injury. The Family Discussion Bureau of the Tavistock Institute of Human Relations, founded by the late Dr Michael Balint (now called Institute of Marital Studies), had recognized a long time ago that, provided such people can contain their sickness within the marital framework, they can not only function within their marriage but they can flourish. To me the work of the Family Discussion Bureau was a serious breakthrough in understanding how people may use their personal problems and contain these within, for example, the marital situation.* As no one is free from *some* injury or conflict, it evolved that human relations and the ability to function well with oneself and in society depended greatly on the availability of such relationships

* Lily Pincus (ed.), *Marriage: Studies in Emotional Conflict and Growth* (London 1960); also Tavistock Institute of Human Relations, *Social Casework in Marital Problems* (London 1955).

(i.e. friendship, marriage, family and other forms of human contacts), in order that one may find a niche for one's pain that is not only acceptable but needed by the other or others.

Having gained a little insight into such human needs, the question then arose, not necessarily or exclusively in human relationships but, say, in the area of work, ambition or finance, whether or not we are in fact driven towards our set goals not by intellectual curiosity alone but by a need to overcome our own perceived or unconscious injuries. *The question of sanity or insanity therefore appeared to depend not so much on the fact of injury in the past but rather on the ability or inability to transform and to use such injury.*

The more I concerned myself with these problems, the more it became apparent that most of us need some hooks in life on to which we can hang our past pains. Having done so, such 'pains' become externalized and give a sense of reassurance or achievement. It was only then that I began to receive some answers to why my comrades in the camp gave up the ghost, committed suicide or became insane. If one takes away from man the last vestige of usefulness (as the SS had done), the last purpose of being alive, then nothing is left except to 'drop out' in some way.

The third way 'out', that is to say in addition to self-destruction and insanity, is anti-social behaviour. Comparatively little has been said in the literature of concentration camps about the extreme cruelty of some prisoners to each other. For example, I could never understand why a medical practitioner, a well-known and respected public figure in my home town, had become a sadist and a murderer within weeks of being in the concentration camp. This man's actions haunted me across the years because I had known him since I was a child. Now, working in Middlesex, my patients had given me a clue as to why, against the background of a useful and decent life, he had become a criminal. When one takes away from, say, a doctor of medicine the possibility of working with his patients, and makes him feel totally and utterly useless in an environment where doctors are needed more than in many other places in the world; when one takes away from such a man the personal relationships -

his wife, his children, his security - and exposes him to completely useless tasks, could it not be that in some cases the internal psychological chemistry will choose an anti-social way 'out' while in others it may choose insanity or self-destruction?

Such thoughts as they emerged, on the evidence that I had heard and witnessed, particularly in relation to the fifty per cent 'failure' group in the Hendon experiment, began to show me that, when satisfactions are almost completely denied, these three choices are in fact the only ones open to man.

If I was right that man tries to work out his injuries in a personally satisfying and socially acceptable way, and succeeding in this becomes a respected member of society, and if, when all these satisfactions are taken away, he can in one way or another become a burden on society, then would it not be logical to assume that most of us who are 'successful' in various endeavours would be entirely unsuccessful if the order of civilization around us were torn to pieces?

But the most disturbing thought, which gave me many sleepless nights when I began to recognize the relevance of satisfactions and frustrations to success and failure in functioning in society, came with the dawning recognition that we can exist as sane or useful people only as long as we can transform and utilize what I would simply term the negative in us. Is it then possible that work and interest, financial security, family relationships, friendships, social contacts and sexuality are all channels or 'containers' through which we can act out our human weaknesses in order to make them appear strengths? If successful transformation or expression of such acting out achieves this end, what then motivates men and women towards achievement of any kind?

For a while one can become rather depressed about the imperfection of the human situation, but eventually it appears that perhaps our growing humanity is dependent on such abreactions. Then the civil servant, politician, doctor, psychotherapist, engineer, skilled worker and many more who get pleasure and satisfaction out of their endeavours may in fact use weakness towards strength. Then love might very well be motivated by some elements of hate. Family life may very well be (and it is) a battleground for finding our identity. Then no friendship is based entirely on love alone, and sexuality may contain a framework in which we can find our hate as well. Freedom then does not exist as yet in the absolute (if it ever will); each man ultimately belongs to no one but himself, and truth and honesty primarily will have to be related to an attempt to be as honest and as truthful as possible with oneself. At the same time, to spell out the total truth to anyone would be so damaging to others that it would be totally unbearable. How could a politician, for example, reveal (even if he had access to the truth about his own motivation) that at least some of the driving force behind his seeking of power is destructive? How could he stand up in a public meeting and say to his electorate: 'If you don't elect me I might easily turn against my wife, children, or society'? I know this is over-simplification, but having examined the lives of so many people, and not least my own, I reluctantly had to come to the conclusion that the difference between Auschwitz and our modern industrial world is only one of degree, a difference that lies basically in the fact that our modern society allows us to find niches, hooks, containers, to transform our bestiality into manhood.

Modern civilized democratic society is still selective as to who can be allowed to become human and who can not. Unemployment is considered a sin even in industrial societies where it is inevitable. There are countries in the world where the economic survival of society is dependent on a large percentage of unemployment, and still the powers that be maintain that it is the fault of the unemployed that they are unemployed. In the camps useless activity destroyed people when every other form of satisfaction had already gone; in our modern society useless activity or, to put it simply, a feeling of uselessness destroys generations of people who have never been given the opportunity of finding alternative 'life tasks' (using Alfred Adler's term) to enable them to feel that they are wanted.

It is not a coincidence that most student unrest occurs in those faculties where there is a great uncertainty among the students as to whether their particular skills will really be needed. Paying people unemployment benefit out of public funds, call it National Assistance, public assistance, Social Security or what you will, makes people feel that they are useless, and useless people will choose one of the three alternatives that were the choice of my comrades in Auschwitz. The welfare state developed a concept of 'looking after people'. This is no doubt needed by those who are physically desperately ill, but even hospitals have realised that the will to live often depends not on first-class medical care but rather on the psychological state of the patient. A will to live is dependent on feeling useful. There is a growing generation of young men and women who sense that they are going to be thrown onto the 'rubbish heap' of society. Again, the welfare state prolongs the adolescent's dependence on the state and then there is no small surprise that, wishing to gain independence and usefulness, these young people turn against the establishment that makes them feel useless.

What is needed is not so much that society should do things for people but that it should at all levels allow people to do things for themselves. We must not create generations of people who will be unable to bear their uselessness. How then can people be useful, and how can we turn the welfare state concept into a concept of self-help?

In therapeutic or preventive terms man must find out, and be helped to find out, how he can use his negative side more constructively. No one can advise on this because no one lives someone else's life. So the task of such preventive therapy and/or education (because the two go hand in hand) is to assist people to find out about themselves and then enable them to make decisions about the route they wish to take which will be useful to them and to society. The methods of treatment described in this book are only pointers to some much larger issues, which extend beyond the principles of psychotherapeutic techniques, prevention, treatment and care.

What prevents the less intelligent from learning skills that will be appropriate expressions of personality, irrespective of whether this would be a commercial proposition or not? Why not allow, or even require, young people to give two years' social service before they enter higher education, and why for that matter is academic achievement still the ultimate goal in our society? Why should social security not be given to people *in order that* they may do and produce things that are not necessarily commercially viable? Perhaps there would be then a return to handicrafts. Why not allow unemployed men, in an age when unemployment figures cannot fail to rise, to earn from whatever they may produce even if the income is not enough to fully maintain them? Why not allow people to learn what they wish to learn, and leave professional education to the few whose 'container' may lie in professions? If society will not sanction the individual's drive towards personal and collective human flourishing, then it may not after all be a bomb that will bring an end to society.

An analysis of the Social Functioning research has been undertaken by Dr Margaret Rodway, of the School of Social Welfare, University of Calgary, Alberta, and will be published shortly.

# 2 The Scale

Apart from the experiences explained in the last chapter, my work with the unemployed taught me a great deal about approaching patients and obtaining information at interviews and made me realize what a great need there was for a system of interviewing that would cover all eventualities but would at the same time give the patient some basic framework to help him explore his life situation.

If a man was sent to me because of problems concerned with unemployment, then all he would talk about was his job and the difficulties stemming from his work, even if it was clear to me that this was only the tip of the iceberg of his emotional problems. Equally, if the same man were to see his general practitioner he would probably not tell him about his work problems even if they had important bearing on his symptoms of ill health. Applicants for state aid were seldom aware that other problems had important bearing on their unemployment. All too often the important aspects of the individual's life were partially or totally cut off from consciousness and the role of the interviewer determined the content of the interview; depending on the label you appeared to have from the client's point of view, you would be given what he thought was appropriate information for those holding that particular label.

Much of this seemed to be the result of years of social conditioning: the patient just could not believe that a local government employee might be interested in him as a *total* person and not just as a man needing financial help. Personal questions were viewed with suspicion, as if they might be a trap. Psychological questions were also viewed with dread. It was new, puzzling and frightening to be asked about one's private affairs on a broader basis. Clearly, it was not going to be easy to get a man who had for years resented authority to be talkative and forthcoming. At first, therefore, I would let the patient talk about whatever he wished until I had gained his confidence. Then, when he felt that I was helping him in what he felt was his main problem, I would cautiously widen the scope of discussion until he brought out his various other emotional dissatisfactions.

It appeared to me that many people had problems that made them feel emotionally dissatisfied and that in order to overcome this feeling they sought some form of external compensation. They might, for example, prowl the city restlessly, hoping to overcome their loneliness in crowded streets and pubs. This seeking for something, yet not knowing what, coupled with a fear of being alone, is one of modern man's greatest problems. One form it takes is always to be changing jobs, always hoping that the next job will be better or will provide greater satisfaction or less loneliness. But the solution to emotional problems cannot be found in the job alone and each time a patient finds this out, he rationalizes his inner fears and anxieties by attacking the nature of his employment and seeking yet another job. Until he gains some insight into some of his emotional (and potential) problems he is unlikely to settle down to any job for any length of time.

I did manage to help some of these men return to work and at the same time to understand that a solution to their problems was not to be found in continual changes of employment and maybe not even in work at all. Having clarified at least one area of their lives they often became aware of marital difficulties, and asked for help in that sphere later when they were back at work. It became increasingly evident that when a man was able to cope with one aspect of his life, he could begin to ask questions and sometimes receive answers about other aspects of it.

I began to realize that I could give the greatest help, obtain the most information and get the best results if I approached my so-called 'patients' in an informal and quasi-social manner, as if I had no label but was just a friendly, thoughtful and knowledgeable fellow citizen. My office must not seem to be either a clinic or a hospital. Yet at the same time I must maintain the balance between being professional and merely social and must try to remain objective in my approach.

My training in psychiatric work had been greatly influenced by the technique as well as the theory of psychoanalysis. I did not however find that this technique was appropriate to the kind of patient I was encountering; on the contrary, many of my patients could be induced to accept help only if it was offered in an informal and quasi-social manner. I felt it was most important to explore ways of helping those very people who, because they were unable to accept the relative impersonality of formal interviews, so often refused to accept psychiatric help until they reached the point of complete breakdown.

New techniques were needed, perhaps based on old psychiatric themes, but adapted to modern problems; and those applying the new techniques must also have a new, wider, much more relaxed approach.

I felt that I must be friend and teacher, listener and talker, lecturer and lectured, passive and often directive, understanding and at times even reproachful; a new brand of specialist, yet at the same time part of the community. At times I had to be the employment agency, marriage guidance council, and even the patient. This was at least how the situation seemed to me when I first struggled with the problem of how people could help themselves most effectively; and yet I was not able to formulate clearly either questions or answers. More and more I was moved to realize that the work that I had carried out with individuals or families was only a small part of the answer. I felt increasingly that my task was to extend some of the awareness I had gained, and the little lessons I had learned, to others who also worked in the community and perhaps had little training in dealing with people. In consequence, I set up training courses, under the umbrella of the Department of Extra-Mural Studies of the University of London, for National Assistance Board managers, executive officers and others. In these courses on human relations I tried to enable people in authority to see how they might appear to those seeking their help; how they might not be given the true information about the problem, not because the client was a liar but because he or she felt that that was all that was expected. I endeavoured to teach them a little about the problems of human behaviour and how to deal more understandingly with the personal difficulties faced by those coming to them for help.

The courses appeared to have considerable practical value, for not only did the students have an opportunity to discuss their clients, and so come to a deeper and perhaps wider understanding of their problems, but they became much more tolerant towards difficult clients when they realized that their aggression was not directed at the students themselves as individuals, nor was it the result of the students' behaviour, but rather stemmed from years of resentment of authority and from disappointment and indignities suffered at the hands of authority figures.

It became clear to me at the end of these courses that teaching these people, whose main function was often to deal with such 'real' situations as poverty, housing and unemployment, presented problems of technique and theory. They were also (like their patients) easily upset by the word 'psychiatric'; so much so that open discussion of many real cases was needed to allay their suspicions. Conversely, once they became enthusiastic about the possibilities of psychological insight into human behaviour they tended to forget that their clients also had 'real' problems which they also had to deal with. Discussions about poverty, housing or work problems must be integrated with personal difficulties if success was to be achieved.

This made it even clearer to me than before that when approaching people with personal emotional problems the government label one was wearing in itself made difficulties for both sides. And it brought home to me the need for much more objective methods of analysing people's behaviour.

Another influence on my thinking at this time was the behaviour of the Hungarian refugees who came over to England after the Hungarian Revolution. Being Hungarian myself I was asked to assist them, especially those who found adjustment to an alien culture difficult and who temporarily showed considerable emotional problems while so doing.

What interested me was the importance to these deeply upset people of a logical link with the past. To a new immigrant trying hard to adapt to a new country, the past is both a problem and a great source of strength. A satisfactory childhood and past home life stands one in good stead. These immigrants longed for their homes; they did not want to be disloyal to their old way of life by adapting too quickly. Yet they had come determined to fit into the English way of life. In adapting they felt unconsciously unfaithful to their old home, which created a mental tug of war within them. When they were ill or under great mental stress they needed memories of the past to give them strength, continuity, reassurance and a tangible link with their old life. Surprisingly, one of the main ways of providing this link was through Hungarian food. Their own kind of food was linked with home, with mother, with security and hope, and in moments of panic it came to assume enormous significance.

This need for a logical consistent link with the past, with the original security of home and parents, might I felt be common to all those suffering from emotional stress. Moreover, it was clear that if early experiences had been satisfying then present problems could be more easily faced.

Slowly I began to bring all my experiences together into a synthesis. My own memories of concentration camps and my knowledge gained from the Hungarian refugees had shown me the relevance of the past in helping those living in a difficult present; my work with the unemployed had shown me the need for financial security, and the need to balance present satisfactions and frustrations. My work with marital problems, whenever they cropped up, had shown me the importance of family relationships, sex and friendship. Throughout, I was all too well aware of the many difficulties connected with interviewing.

It became clear that too low a level of satisfaction and too much frustration prevented the individual from working as part of society. But in which area of his life did the crux of the problem lie? How could one diagnose this and then remedy the result?

What I wished to evolve was a tool that would measure the relationship of satisfaction and frustration as experienced by the individual at any given moment in time. This would give me some idea of how he was functioning in society. The idea of social functioning - which in basic terms is what I was interested in - was not new and has been discussed by several authors for the last two decades or more; indeed, its basic concepts derive from years of experiment, research and practice. But what I was after was a *practical* approach, which would integrate method and theory in a particular practice and would assist a patient to integrate and to use his experience in a way that would be perceived by him as new and creative. Its main focus would be on the *positive,* and on how frustrations, abnormalities and difficulties could be turned into ultimate gain. My idea was not original in itself but rather was an attempt to integrate various psychotherapeutic methods into a new totality.

There appeared to me to be five main areas of human life in which success or failure manifests itself: (1) in work and interests; (2) in financial security; (3) in friendship and social relationships; (4) in family life; and (5) in sexuality. Frustration also can be seen in five areas: (1) in the blocking or paralysis of activity; (2) in depression; (3) in alienation or feelings of persecution; (4) in somatic or psychosomatic symptoms; and (5) in various forms of escape-route, such as the use of drugs and alcohol and the acting out of fantasies.

Satisfaction is the individual's subjective perception that he is making good use of his potentials. Frustration is the inability to make use of such potentials. Both of these could perhaps be projected onto a scale that would show, not only to the therapist but also to the patient or client, how his subjective human experiences corresponded to the objective reality, his ability or inability to function with others.

Clearly, our first satisfactions depend on the most primary relationship of all, that between mother and child. This relationship provides us with satisfactions in the following areas:

1) security in relation to basic need;
2) sensual pleasure through being fed, caressed, cared for;
3) non-sensual pleasure, i.e. mutual affection;
4) the basis of primary relationship: 'I am not alone, someone is with me';
5) primitive play activities, at first directed mainly towards the mother and later towards toys.

As the child grows older, these original satisfactions are

also found in the outer world, and the ability to find them may depend on the quality of original experience.

1)  security is now represented by income and comforts;
2)  sensual pleasure is represented by sexual satisfactions;
3)  mutual affection and ability to love grow, for example, through and with the partner in marriage and children;
4)  the primary relationship extends to include a circle of friends;
5)  play activities are represented in terms of meaningful and creative work and/or hobbies.

Thus society and all that it can offer would become (or so I saw it then) an extension of the mother and would continue what she started; but if she failed too massively in one or more of these areas the individual's capacity to find all these satisfactions elsewhere was likely to be impaired.

It was then for the first time that I devised a very basic and simple scoring system of satisfaction and frustration. My hypothesis was that man can function in society only if half of the above named satisfactions are fulfilled.

The human relations courses were still going on, and each year added something new to their content. So, having arrived at my first primitive assessment of satisfaction and frustration, I asked my students in these courses to test this hypothesis by assessing the amount of satisfaction or dissatisfaction under each heading of a provisional points system. Each definite answer 'yes' scored 20 points; an answer with some doubt 10 points; and a definite 'no' answer scored zero. It then became clear that very few people function at 100 per cent level or, to be more precise, at a level of 100 points. But many contented people did function at a level of 70/80 points. Frustration seemed bearable around 60 points but the score between 50 and 60 indicated that both the interviewee and the interviewer became aware of quite serious problems and conflicts, although the interviewee could still help himself. Any score under 50 seemed to correlate with social or mental illness. I noticed also some significance in the fact that young people between twenty-five and thirty-five seemed to have scored less than 'normal' people between thirty-five and forty-five. People of sixty-five years or over also seemed to have scored somewhat less. For example it seemed then that a score of 50 might be quite normal at twenty-five and quite abnormal at forty-five.

It was clear from this that if a man scored under 50 points and was to be rehabilitated, become adjusted to society and find meaningful work, then his total score of satisfaction would have to be increased by 10 to 20 points. It would not matter in which area these extra points occurred: if his marriage was unhappy and he earned little but his hobbies, children, friends and work were sufficiently rewarding, he would manage. On the other hand if all his satisfactions came from outside work, he might prefer to live on the dole. Clearly, this was one of many aspects which would have to be looked into further.

In 1962 Dr Davis, a GP, and I tried to find out more about the scale of social functioning. Five areas were studied: finance; sex; primary and secondary family relationships; friendship, work and/or outside interests. Five questions were devised for each area. The responses would be positive, negative or uncertain, scoring 4, 0 and 2 respectively.

Thus in any one area the maximum possible score would be 20, but by omitting the count on any 2 scored the lower figure would be reached, the difference between the two scores being the index of uncertainty. The score would then be expressed as, for example 12/16, indicating three positive and two uncertain replies. The individual area scores were added together giving an overall maximum of 100, and scores below 60 demonstrated lack of satisfaction.

A small pilot scheme was then tried out on 238 people: samples came from Dr Barnardo's Homes, family service units, mental health departments, the probation service, church-goers and non-church-goers. While we were well aware that the groups were too small to be of any real statistical significance, we felt nevertheless that a number of conclusions might justifiably be drawn from them. What we did find was that a sense of satisfaction is no guide in itself to the level of achievement as measured by the criteria of our society. The same qualities that enable a man or woman to function adequately in a competitive and acquisitive society are not necessarily the same as those that help them to achieve satisfaction. It was clear that the ability to function adequately in society is related to the aggregate scores in the five areas. Where the scores are high there are some reserves, and these individuals should be able to weather storms of everyday life. If the total score is in the low 60s people may very well break down into subjective stressful changes. Furthermore, the likelihood of breakdown has increased if the stress is applied to an already low-scoring area. This immediately raised the question of the value of the scale in detecting danger areas in borderline groups.

I soon realized that a lack of satisfaction as presented on the scale developed thus far did not give a clear indication as to the nature of frustration. Therefore I designed a frustration or negative index, which also consisted of twenty-five questions and covered such areas as paralysis of activity, alienation or persecution, depression, somatic or psychosomatic syndromes and various forms of escape-routes such as the use of drugs and alcohol. The scoring was identical with that of the satisfaction scale, i.e. 4 — 0, corresponding to the 'yes', 'perhaps', and 'no' answers.

Immediately following the negative index, which I arrived at through clinical considerations, the final part of the present scale of social functioning was devised and copyrighted in 1967 in its present form. This last part included a synthesis scale evaluating past, present and future aspirations, consisting of five questions scored on feeling tone between 0 and 20. For example, 'How far have you achieved your ambition in life?' is scored from 0 (not at all) to 20 (completely).

The positive, negative and synthesis scores had now given us an opportunity to sharpen our diagnostic knowledge, and the scale was sent for various validations which subsequently have been, and are being, undertaken in this country and abroad. Furthermore, we found that the most relevant part of this developed scale was its therapeutic value to the client himself. No other scale was to such an extent a sharing device between therapist and client. Together now the client and the social worker can explore, through the use of the scale, the present pattern of satisfactions and frustrations, and together they can identify areas that are felt by the client to be most crippling or most hopeful. The scale thus offers the client the opportunity for self-observation within a *safe structure,* a starting point for his self-examination and subsequent actions to be taken, and, after having achieved some changes, a return to the structure to observe the change *de facto* on the scale itself.

Initially, the solutions are by no means perfect, but often it can be the beginning of a better level of overall functioning. By reflection, what has previously been experienced by the patient as 'internal' is now 'externalized', and through this process of self-examination and self-observation he can clarify some of his problems or at least find a different way of perceiving them, and he may recognize how his life patterns are interconnected. He can, perhaps for the first time, ask himself clearly relevant questions about his life and attempt to formulate answers to such questions. If he is successful in doing this, a restless urge will enable him to act differently in life, an urge that is due to the fact that the so-far useless experiences of his life have become more meaningful and useful. In short, through this method he can begin to have access to his own resources, which so far have been partially or totally blocked.

Many clients had suffered for years from overwhelming frustration in several areas of their life: they had become unable to make a satisfying use of their experiences. So their therapy concentrated on the expression of some form of creativity: on doing something which they themselves found useful. Creativity depends both on the range of opportunities that society offers and on society's acceptance of unusual or deviant behaviour. Most people who function adequately in society have found some solution to the creative use of their frustrations. Aggression, for example, may be used in many socially accepted ways. If it is so used then it does not show itself as a symptom. If the individual has no such ways of expressing his aggression then it becomes symptomatic because he uses it in an unacceptable way which often causes him and society distress.

For example most people who like their jobs find outlets in them through which they can externalize aspects of themselves that could be self-destructive. The lawyer who defends, the surgeon who operates, the reporter who moves with his camera into danger spots, the butcher who cuts up meat, the man in a humdrum job with many outside hobbies: all these people are channelling negative energies into positive ones. They have learned to live with their frustrations: pain has become their spur. The surgeon who may consciously choose his professional tool, the knife, to help suffering people may have a hidden motive to hurt, to injure. But this hidden (and therefore unacceptable) desire is being transformed into something positive and acceptable when he operates on a patient.

The basic issue, therefore, is not *why* aggression exists, but rather in what way it is being used, or even more precisely, whether or not the individual has a choice in his utilization of this *potential*.

So far, psychotherapy has attempted to move the client away from any kind of deviancy. We have found, however, that we must confront our clients with what they experience as abnormal, pathological or symptomatic. This method of confrontation of that aspect within themselves that seems painful, frustrating or defeating, we call the 'dialogue'. Confrontation with what people experience as negative, or what society may consider negative, often releases hidden human potential that is locked up in those very areas we tended to consider needing modification, change or interpretation.

Eventually the scale was applied to over a thousand people, most of whom were managing normally in society at the time, were aware that they had problems but had not sought outside help. It was clear that the scale was a most useful and helpful tool for them. Ordinary people had been able to grasp the basic concept of social functioning and use its insights to help themselves. Patients felt that they had been given a new and useful way of looking at their problems; interviewers felt that they could reach the core of the problem quicker and could get their patients to tackle difficulties co-operatively. Both sides could examine the situation objectively and discuss where and what had broken down with mutual understanding.

Moreover, instead of interviewing patients for nine or more hours, clear objective communication was established quickly and a profile of the problems could be obtained in about one hour. This profile could then be transferred to another interviewer or case-worker if necessary without difficulty. This was extremely useful in the case of rapid staff changes or holiday periods. The scale provided a common language between workers so that a patient's problems could be conveyed concisely, on one sheet of foolscap paper, from one individual to another without misunderstanding and without too much subjective distortion.

The scale was also very useful as a teaching tool to help new young students to be concise and objective. Furthermore, it proved strikingly useful in work with young adolescents as it enabled them to see their current situation clearly and to see where their understanding and experience needed strengthening.

From research carried out it was clear that those with adequate resources to meet crises could function normally but that some groups were at risk in a crisis unless adequately supported, while those needing most care could barely cope from one day to the next and needed constant help. Crisis points arose at moments of change: either outer change such as starting school, work or a new job, marriage, parenthood or retirement; or inner developmental change such as in adolescence, pregnancy, old age or at times of illness. Once the pattern of satisfaction and frustration had been seen in a family at risk it was possible to work out when they would need positive active support and indeed to help them to see when they would need it and what shape it would take. This education in a new kind of self-help, born of understanding of one's own personal pattern of satisfaction and frustration, was of immense potential value.

# 3 The Initial Interview

The initial interview is the first step in the treatment process, as it lays down the foundation of relationships, attitudes and the respective roles of patient and therapist. The decision to seek professional help outside one's own environment and resources is, psychologically, a part of the meeting with the 'helping' professional. In a sense, therefore, the road towards a meeting is already *the* meeting. When I decide (or am being persuaded) that I need outside help, I have acknowledged that the problem is much greater than my ability to cope with it. The delegation of responsibility invariably creates some ambivalence in relation to and towards the 'helping' professional who, more often than not, is as yet no more than a name, with an address and a professional status. My failure to cope with some painful aspect(s) of my life creates in me a feeling of dependence in relation to the as-yet unknown professional, with an accompanying resentment and - depending on the extent of my regression - an unrealistic expectation of him. Such an emotional state sets a ready canvas for further projection (and transference) when the actual meeting does take place.

The therapist has chosen his profession (among other reasons) to satisfy his own emotional need(s) in relation to and *through* the patient. What kind of satisfaction does he hope to achieve for himself through this other human being who is in pain? Apart from his conscious wish to 'help the patient to grow' (one customary reason given for motivation), what is there *for him* in the growth of the other? Has he chosen his profession (among some other more rational reasons) because he needs to grow through and with the patient? Such and similar emotions may set a ready canvas for projection and transference onto the patient when the actual meeting does take place.

Before any meeting between 'helper' and 'the one needing help', there seems to be a mutuality of interest between the two: the patient needs the therapist for his growth (represented in the present by his inability to cope with life, or with some aspect of it), and the therapist needs the patient for his own growth (represented by his need to be needed). It may very well be that, without the patient, the therapist would be unable to cope with his own life, or some aspect of it, and would need help to explore ways and means in which his need to be needed would be actualized. *The treatment process therefore can be successful only if two people with their own particular problems decide to use each other's presence and experience towards their own unique solution and growth.*

Emotional needs are independent of academic or intellectual preparation for professional discipline or practice; the former define the common humanity on which the latter will have to be based. The emerging 'peer-relationship' is based on the commonalty of the human condition; it does not expect commonalty of roles. Without a defined 'role expectation' the therapist cannot carry out the disciplined practice to enable the patient to become his *own* examiner, rather than both he and the therapist feeling that he is under examination.

It is well known in psychoanalytical literature that our personal problems enter into our attitudes towards others, that our likes and dislikes for other people contain elements of our own personal emotional difficulties. Unless one is aware of this, one may be unable to stand outside the patient's world and so help him objectively with his problems. Not only does projection onto someone else exist, but there is also introjection, when one takes certain problems of other people within oneself and fails to recognize that their problems are similar to one's own.

A student in training talked about an interview he had had with a married couple. He had found the woman easy to get on with 'because of her free flow of emotions'. But he found the husband a 'very difficult character indeed'. On being asked why this man was so difficult, he said that he was self-assured and quite unable to share his feelings. The student was then encouraged to look at the wife's problem as if it were his own. In short, it was found that the student had in himself something of the husband's emotional patterns. It was quickly brought home to him that, while he could be very free with his own emotions when with people who were not close to him, he too showed lack of feeling with those that mattered. It was then necessary for the student to examine this aspect of himself very carefully and in depth so that in future he would be more understanding of those similar to himself. (It turned out that the student's emotional problems stemmed from a fear of being abandoned, which had made him build up defences against those he loved.)

It is not claimed that the interview in social functioning is new or original. It derives from existing methods and principles with a view to making the patient feel at ease with the therapist and not under any kind of 'parental examination'. The therapist will not convey to his patient the idea that he knows more about him than he does know. There is no 'ah-ha!' response whereby one indicates a greater understanding of the patient's situation than the patient is capable of stating. In fact it may very well be that both therapist and patient will be at a loss to know for some time what it is that the patient is trying to communicate; it is not in the least important that the therapist should understand, but it is very important that the *patient* should understand. In this approach the only understanding required from the therapist is to know what the patient has understood and stated about his life. The therapist's task is to enter not his own but the patient's understanding. Even before the initial interview it is important for the therapist to develop an attitude that allows the patient to feel, behave and act as a responsible adult, even if this is at times difficult for both of them. This responsibility should create a dynamic and creative interview situation. Such responsible behaviour within the interview situation comes about in a short space of time only if the therapist denies himself the pleasure of the 'ah-ha' effect and resigns from his wish to interpret the *other* according to learned knowledge, insight and intuition, and if he refrains from giving *his* interpretation to the patient. He must not jump to conclusions and then push his perceptions onto the patient.

The initial interview lays down the foundation of this 'self-creating' process and consists of some interconnected phases, but there is no hard and fast rule as to its order:

1) statement by the patient of his life situation and/or pressing problems;
2) skilled summaries by the therapist as to his understanding of the patient's stated situation;
3) teaching the patient to 'capsulate' or conceptualize his statement into short and meaningful summaries;
4) beginning of the process of self-observation, when patient creates a theme or themes from his recorded summaries (through writing them down or using a tape-recorder);
5) discussion of possible immediate action(s) as to change of frustration into creativity.

## The patient's statement

The purpose and function of this exposé is that the patient should express his experienced life-situation, painful or otherwise, in order to free himself in some measure from the pressures that are at present weighing him down, and by sharing his experiences 'unload' these on to another human being. He may, as previously stated, have an unrealistic expectation and resentment of the therapist. On the other hand he may expect that the 'talking cure' will in fact lead to miraculous solutions; alternatively, he may hold back because he does not really wish anyone else to come up with solutions.

The patient should be allowed to make this statement without any unnecessary interruption from the therapist, even if the latter does not fully understand what is being said to him. The only exception to this rule is a situation in which the patient has great difficulty in communicating. Only then will the therapist, through questioning and through focusing on particular issues, help the patient with the process of communication. During the first ten or fifteen minutes, therefore, only the patient 'has the floor', the therapist remaining a friendly listener. If during this time the patient shows signs of distress or any other affective behaviour, the therapist may show through his *spontaneous* affective reactions that he is not just listening but also intensely *feeling* with him. The non-formulated message is: 'You are not alone; I am with you.' This is very different from some therapeutic techniques where the therapist must, at all cost, remain outside the patient's emotions. For a human being to remain outside the experiences of another could be considered inhuman, or at least non-caring, by the patient. *The therapist's silence should serve no other purpose, therefore, than to encourage the patient's free flow of communication.*

Another purpose of the patient's statement is that he should · experience in these moments the macrocosm of his existence. The microcosm of the present essentially contains aspects of past totality. The meaning of this particular experience will, however, be manifest in retrospect only at a later part of the interview. At this stage the following inter-merging emotional patterns may be felt by the patient: some (even minute) relief at being able to share himself with the therapist; a feeling that he is not alone with his pain and pleasure; a feeling of being overwhelmed by his life-experiences; hope that the therapist will solve his problem by some miracle; resentment of the therapist.

## The therapist's summaries

It will be remembered that until this point the patient is still in a state of regression, although the therapist's spontaneous affective responses may have broken the ice a little. The purpose of the summary is to convey to the patient that what he has said has been understood by the therapist, and also that the patient may discover that these summaries do in fact 'add up to something'.

The timing of summaries is of great importance. Although no hard and fast rule may be made, some natural intervals do seem to occur when the patient's flow of communication comes to a temporary halt, and summaries may then be attempted. As these summaries are of very great importance in the therapeutic process, the therapist will make his intention clear to the patient:

Perhaps at this point you will allow me to try to put together what you have said so far, as I would like to be sure that I have understood what you have told me. Please do correct me if what I sum up is not what you have said.

Summarizing requires considerable skill, but it can be learned only over a period of time. It must always be clear and brief, using as much of and as often as possible the patient's own words. *It requires disciplined memory through skilful selection of relevant data by avoiding many details.*

During the first summary the patient is usually in agreement. He would, as yet, not contradict the therapist. During subsequent summaries, however, he will increasingly attempt correction. Once this takes place, regression gives way to more mature feelings. *The patient's contradiction of the therapist is the first important step in the treatment process and lays down the foundation of a 'peer-relationship' between them; it also activates some feeling of self-effectiveness in the patient.*

All summaries are related to the content of the material (to what the patient has *said*) and not to observation as to the delivery of the content (for example the way in which the patient has said it). Such observations may be forthcoming from the patient himself at a later point of the interview, when he has learned some measure of self-observation and has excluded his feelings of being observed.

## Teaching the patient to 'capsulate' or conceptualize

The therapist will soon notice the effect on the patient of such summaries. If the effect is considerable (and it often is) the therapist may then proceed to encourage the patient to attempt from time to time to formulate his own summaries. If no such effect is manifest such conceptualization or auto-summary should not be attempted, or should at least be postponed to subsequent interview or interviews. In crisis situations the patient is often so overwhelmed by his problems that he may find it impossible to become an observer of his own feelings and actions. In such a situation the therapist, while still carrying on with his own occasional summaries, will refrain from asking the patient to do the same until this becomes feasible at another point of time, perhaps during another interview.

If the patient is prepared and ready for such self-summaries the therapist may ask him to write them down after their verbal statement, or he may use a small tape-recorder. As the purpose of these summaries is to assist the patient in the process of self-observation, some find the writing down and reading back more meaningful than hearing a playback from the recorder. Some patients who are more 'auditive' find the playing back method more effective. There are also some who prefer both.

Many people, however, for a variety of reasons (intelligence, education, fear of commitment), have difficulty in conceptualizing and prefer to delegate such responsibility to the therapist. In this case it will become the latter's task to 'capsulate' relevant parts of the interview and record them for and/or with the patient. When this happens, as has been said before, the therapist will make sure that such summaries are a true mirror of the *patient's* statements. In such situations it is important for the therapist to point out the reason(s) for undertaking this exercise. If anything is written down it should immediately be shared with the patient. Preferably the seating arrangement should be such that the patient is able to observe the process of written recording. If a tape-recorder is used the therapist will explain to the patient that such recordings will be erased at the conclusion of the interview, if possible during the patient's presence. The recordings will be kept only if the patient wishes to have further access to them (for example, he may wish to take the cassette home with him, or to refer to it at a later point of treatment). Many patients, however, learn to capsulate their statement during the initial interview, and usually find this very reassuring.

## The onset of self-observation

Man has many more resources within his past experience than he is using at any given time. This assumption is, of course, more applicable to people who feel, at the point when seeking outside help, that they have no resources left at all. Paralysis of human functioning is the result of a series of unsuccessful attempts to cope with the experiences of living; it follows that most people who feel themselves to be failures are conditioned to perceive themselves as such. No human life in its continuum consists of frustration alone.

Lack of present self-effectiveness, however, may focus both intellectual and emotional attention on the negative aspects of living, and may create an illusion of global failure. As this view is more often than not being presented at the initial interview, it is the therapist's task to help the patient to develop a somewhat more balanced view of himself. This can be achieved only if the patient is allowed to reflect on what he has said (and beyond his statement are his feelings and his actions), and if he can deduce from this (as represented by a series of capsulated summaries) some theme or themes that are meaningful to him. *The capsulated summaries are containers that are now viewed by the patient from outside his stated experiences.* As he struggles to arrive at a theme or message he is able to use more of his total experiences than he could before conditioning to failure had occurred. The realization that there appears to be some meaningful message hidden among those summaries, which he might use outside the consulting room, often gives him a feeling of hope coupled with impatience to 'get on with it'. As the initial interview is at no time a platform for interpersonal discussion with the therapist, but rather a concentration on the patient's 'outer' life situation, he cannot use his relationship with the therapist to delay action *outside* the consulting-room. At this juncture both hope and a great deal of tension is being experienced by the patient. *It is this tension that will motivate him into subsequent action in an attempt to cope with his life problems once more.*

### Discussion of possible action(s)

So far, the initial interview may be instrumental in bringing about the following:

1) reducing regression by focusing on the patient's stated problem(s) as he perceives them;

2) helping the patient to realize, however painful and/or confusing his life-situation may be in the 'here and now', that it can be stated and that it is, more often than not, meaningful;

3) indicating (via the summaries) that the therapist does understand him and that he too may understand such

summaries and the theme or 'message' emerging from them (this may give him a growing feeling of self-effectiveness);

4) activation of a former, more global, life-experience, which hitherto was not accessible to the patient because the focus of his attention was on the present, often confusing, issues;

5) imparting some feeling of hope and impatience to do something about his problems;

6) a peer-relationship (the non-utilization of transference), freeing the patient to use his pent-up psychic energy outside the consulting-room;

7) the possibility of discussing alternative actions.

At the conclusion of the initial interview it is of the greatest importance that the therapist should know what *kind* of action the patient has in mind to free himself from his impatience or tension. There can be possible difficulties ahead for the patient unless some of his intentions are viewed and discussed together with the therapist. Great skill is needed to help to direct the patient's psychic energies towards positive rather than negative ventures. If the patient indicates during this discussion that his planned action is to be destructive, the therapist will offer him alternatives and explain to him the reasoning behind the offered alternatives. In any case, the therapist can offer him the opportunity to discuss such alternatives during some subsequent interviews, as it is unlikely that one interview alone can explore all possible alternatives.

*Initial Interview with Mr X (case 1)*
This fifty-two-year-old man contacted me by letter. The letter simply said that: 'after what others might consider to be a successful life, I have reached the end of the road. I don't know where I have lost my turning.' He asked me to see him, and a week later I did so.

He was a tall, thin man, with scanty greyish hair. He was trying to be very controlled, but was visibly nervous and frightened of me and of the interview. His accent and manner betrayed his education and background. Born in New

Zealand, his parents brought him over to England when he was three years old.

The following is a shortened version of our initial interview.

*Mr X* The traffic is becoming quite awful in London; six or seven years ago I could have covered this distance in half the time. I am terribly grateful to you for giving up your time . . . I must confess I find this quite an ordeal. You see, I am not very good at sharing my thoughts with others . . . yet this is why I really came to see you. It is like a bleak depression . . . feeling quite unsafe, I suppose. Where would you like me to begin?

*E. H.* You have already made a start. I know it is difficult. Some years ago I felt depressed too.

*Mr X* Did you really? You too have been depressed?

*E. H.* Yes. I was very depressed.

*Mr X* Did it take you a long time to overcome it?

*E. H.* Some time, but it worked in the end. What I would like you to do is to share with me what your situation is at present. Just go ahead, and here and there I will check with you that I really understand what you are sharing with me. Tell me anything you wish.

*Mr X* There are so many things - where does one really start? Well . . . I said in my letter that I have reached a kind of cul-de-sac. That's how I really feel. A kind of brick wall. I am an accountant; financially I am not doing badly at all, but for the last few years I have hated every moment of it. When I get up in the morning I feel more exhausted than at the end of a long day. The only thing that seems to help a little is music, but now I haven't even the energy to go to concerts. The children are grown up; Timothy is at university - he is the eldest, twenty-two next spring. Philip has just got his A levels and in the autumn he will probably go to medical school; he has wanted to be a doctor ever since he entered grammar school. Louise hopes to enter your profession if she does well next year. I suppose she will. They all seem to know where they are going . . . by the way, Timothy wants to go into the television business, producing or something . . . . Considering everything, we haven't made a bad business with our children; we have had no real trouble with them; perhaps Timothy was a bit difficult at times - long hair, you know . . . some strange company and the rest of it. Yet he too seems to be shaping up - has a lot of idealism and doesn't quite know what to do with it. He went to public school and managed to put up with the discipline there, but just about . . . I wanted to send Philip there too, but my wife . . . thought he would do well in a state school, so he went there and did better in a sense than Timothy. I don't really know if these things are relevant at all . . . I mentioned my wife. She is my age - we have been married now for twenty-five years. It is difficult to put it into words - we are all right, and yet something isn't quite right. Nowadays there is so much talk about sex and things - well, that part of our relationship died some years ago. I couldn't tell you how it happened. She has been very good with the children; they always came first. I suppose that's right. We talk about things, yet not about things that matter - to me. I must admit that she is more energetic than I am. Lately she has been busying herself with stamps - not just collecting the damn things but she goes twice a week and helps at a stamp-collector's. They buy and sell stamps. I thought it an odd thing for a woman to do, but there you are!

*E. H.* Will you allow me to try to summarize what you have said so far, as I would like to make sure that I have understood what you have told me? Please do correct me if what I say is not what you have told me.

*Mr X* Please.

*E. H.* You said, if I have understood you, that you have a kind of bleak depression and some feeling of not being safe. Your work does not give you satisfaction and you feel tired most of the time. Your children have now grown up, and are on the whole doing quite well. They have some aim in life, they know where they are going. You have been married for twenty-five years and your relationship with your wife is all right but your sexuality died some time ago and you don't share the same interests.

*Mr X* Yes. What you have said is quite correct - quite. Yet, how can my relationship with Mary be all right if sexually and interest-wise we are now apart?

(Long silence)

There is also something else. Oh, it must be three or four years ago that I met someone at Queen Elizabeth Hall. It was after the concert and we were coming down the stairs. She was much younger than I; in her early thirties or so. As I learned later, she had been divorced for some time, and she worked for a large firm as a high-powered secretary. Well, what in fact happened was that for the first time since my marriage I entertained a young lady for a light meal. I found her very attractive and we seemed to share a great deal. Yes indeed, I must say we had a great deal in common. Then we met quite regularly, at least once a week - had dinner together, went to concerts and the rest . . . (silence) I remember it was early spring when one night she asked me to have coffee with her at her flat. By now she knew that I was married and, although I did not speak a great deal to her about Mary, she must have known that something wasn't quite right between us. It's an odd thing, you know; even now, as I am recalling those events and telling you that she must have gathered that something wasn't quite right between Mary and myself, it hurts me to say these things. Half the trouble with me is, I think, that I simply turn my head away from what really hurts me. I knew then, as I know now, that our marriage had been on the rocks really in more ways than one; yet to admit this fully filled me then, as it fills me now, with great horror. I suppose I want things to be the way I wish them to be.

Now I seem to have lost my trian of thought - oh yes, it was a classical situation. A middle-aged man, misunderstood by his wife, spending an evening in the flat of a young woman. I couldn't make love to her. I tried desperately but it simply just did not work out - I felt awful. I can't tell you, Professor, how terrible I really felt. I don't think she took it half as seriously as I did - the whole episode. That night when I drove home, I seriously thought of committing suicide.

*E. H.* Again, allow me to try to sum up. Again, please correct me if what I am saying is not what you have told me. You have said that you were puzzled about your sentence as to how you can have a reasonable relationship with your wife if sexually and interest-wise you seem to be apart . . .

*Mr X* Sorry to interrupt you. I did not say that my relationship with Mary is reasonable; I thought I said that it was all right; and another thing - somehow your word 'puzzled' doesn't really express what I am feeling. It's more than being puzzled.

*E. H.* May I correct myself then. You said that your relationship was all right with your wife, yet how could this be if sexually and, as you put it, interest-wise, you are apart?

*Mr X* That's quite right.

*E. H.* You then went on to say that you met a young woman some years ago, found her attractive in more ways than one, and after seeing her for some time, eventually you attempted to make love to her and failed in this attempt. You felt awful about this and thought of committing suicide afterwards.

*Mr X* Yes. It adds up to that; but we must add to what you have said something that I feel is rather important: my inherent inability to see things as they really are, yet secretly knowing that they are as they are.

*E. H.* Would you like to write down some of your comments, summaries, and reflections, Mr X? It might help at the end of our meeting to see what we have covered here today. I could also use this small tape-recorder for our summaries . . . whichever you like.

*Mr X* I would rather write them down.

*E. H.* All right. Would it be possible for you to put down, then, what you have just said? If I remember correctly, you said . . .

*Mr X* I have an inherent inability to face things as they are, yet I know somehow that those things are still there.

*E. H.* Please write this down on this paper.

*Mr X* As I have written it down now, I see how woolly it all sounds.

*E. H.* Well, how would you make it more concise?

Mr X for some minutes stared into nothingness, thinking very hard. Then he wrote on the paper and said: 'Right, I think I have got it now.'

*E. H.* Could you share with me, Mr X, what you have written down?

*Mr X* My marriage has been lousy for years. It was all right, perhaps, for the children, but not for me. I closed my eyes to my problems with Mary; mixed up her being a good mother with her being a lousy wife. She has been dutiful to me but not loving.

(He added after some reflection:)

You know what. I really feel very angry now with her. I suppose I should write this down too?

*E. H.* Yes.

*Mr X* You see, after that fiasco, I have never met that young woman again. I was quite convinced that I was finished. Since then I have considered myself a failure in everything. Truly, if you come to think of it, I was around at home just to look after the family. You know what children are like; they give back very little. I don't mean material things, of course; I am speaking about feelings. My daughter Louise is perhaps the only one who really cares for me. I don't want to sound as if I am sorry for myself, but hell, in a sense I am. There is that stupid bastard, milked by everyone, and what does he get out of life? Nothing! Now how am I going to sum this up?

(Long silence, while trying to sort out his thoughts and feelings. Then he reads it back to me:)

While I looked after my family's well-being no one, apart from my daughter, really looked after what I needed. I feel it's sad.

(After a pause he added:)

. . . and it makes me angry, too.

(Then he went on:)

There are so many things I wished to do when I was young. I wanted to become a pianist, but my parents weren't interested at all. At university I discovered that I could write, in fact I edited a maga-zine for some time. I even had a flair for painting - nothing special, though. My job brings me into contact with a lot of people, but work-ing out other people's financial affairs very much limits the scope of such relationships. I don't really know whether I am all that interested in other people. I have a very poor view of humanity in any case. Yet there must be something in me that kept me going throughout all these years . . . but what?

*E. H.* Would you like to sum up what you have just said?

*Mr X* Oh God, this will be difficult.

*E. H.* Please try.

(Three or four minutes' pause, before Mr X began to write again:)

*Mr X* I have had some artistic flair, perhaps even more than that, but I was prevented from exploring this. On the whole, people disappoint me. Something keeps me alive but I don't know what.

(Then after a brief moment or two he added:)

What I find quite interesting about this writing bit is that really my whole life is here in front of me. I don't quite know why but I feel quite good about it all.

*E. H.* You see, Mr X, that is really the whole point of the exercise. We are often so much caught up in the mechanics of living that we seldom have an opportunity to reflect on what it all adds up to. What you and I are doing now is to take stock and then see where to go from here. What I would like to do now is to look at these summaries and try to arrive at a theme or themes, so that at least we have something to start with. Now let us see what we have got so far. Please read through your notes and read them to me.

*Mr X* (reading aloud:) I have an inherent inability to face things as they are, yet I know somehow that those things are still there. My marriage has been lousy for years. It was all right, perhaps, for the children, but not for me. I closed my eyes to my problems with Mary; mixed up her being a good mother with her being a lousy wife. She has been dutiful to me but not loving. I really feel very angry with her. While I looked after my family's well-being no one, apart from my daughter, really looked after what I needed. I feel it's sad. I have had some artistic flair, perhaps even more than that, but I was prevented from exploring this. On the whole, people disappoint me. Something keeps me alive but I don't know what.

Having read these summaries, Mr X once more stared at no-where for what seemed a very long time. I did not interrupt him, nor was I anxious to help him at this juncture. At times he would casually look at the paper in front of him, and then his eyes would wander away. He had hardly looked at me during this time. He was, so it seemed, alone with his life, or at least with those aspects of it that he had stated significantly and recorded. Then he turned towards me:

*Mr X* What is it really that you want me to do now?

*E. H.* I would like you to see whether those summaries contain some message or theme that you can express. In a sense I would like to do a summary of those summaries.

(He looked me straight in the eye and said:)

*Mr X* This is the most difficult of all so far.

*E. H.* I know it is, yet it is important that you should try.

(He was now carefully studying the paper. Again minutes passed by. Then he said:)

*Mr X* There is a great deal missing from my life; things that are not here.

*E. H.* I know that, but you can only sum up what you have got.

I knew that this was the most difficult part for him; for that matter, it is the most difficult part for anyone during the initial interview. Sometimes patients need a great deal of encouragement to arrive at some kind of synthesis. Mr X, however, needed no further help from me. He began slowly but quite deliberately:

*Mr X* What I see clearly emerging is that I seem to be blaming others for my impotence. I use this word to express my whole situation. What has carried me so far, and still does, is the secret hope that I can become potent. If I wanted to be even more precise I would say: I have allowed myself to become a cog and I did not want to acknowledge it.

(Without any further request from me, he wrote down the last sentence on the paper.)

*E. H.* Now we have arrived at some theme. Where do we go from here?

*Mr X* I must try to sort out the mess, starting with Mary.

*E. H.* How would you start?

(He now seemed very definite:)

*Mr X* I must tell her how I really feel, what I really am. That's where I shall start.

(Then after a minute's reflection:)

I don't know whether you can resurrect something that has been dead for years - my marriage I mean - but then there may be some miracles round the corner; I don't know! It may even be that Mary would want to see you too. I really don't know. But I have to start there.

And that was the end of my initial interview with Mr X.

To conclude: Mr X saw me on two more occasions some months later. His wife did not wish to see me and did not, or could not, build bridges to save the marriage. It is sad that after twenty-five years a marriage should terminate in divorce, but this is what happened in this case. Mr X is now married again to a woman only a few years younger than himself. They live outside London and there seems to be a great deal of warmth and love between them. While still carrying out his professional work as an accountant, Mr X took some painting courses and now paints for his own pleasure. Both husband and wife go regularly to concerts, and have a small but intimate circle of friends. Mr X's secret hope of potency has become a reality.

## Summary notes on the initial interview

The initial interview is the foundation of the relationship with the patient, and also creates the climate for all subsequent treatment sessions. The patient will recall his life-situation in the present and, through a process of self-observation (summaries, playback) may utilize his experiences from his past. As the latter include a wide spectrum of past feelings, actions and thoughts, the initial interview activates past experiences (even if details of these are hidden) so that problems in the present may be coped with more creatively. The past is often conditioned by failure in the present and consists of patterns of success and failure, and can thus give the patient a more balanced view of his total life situation.

When past knowledge is not available to a person, the (negative) powers of the unconscious may turn against him; but when the past becomes accessible the unconscious becomes more of an ally and less of an enemy. The time interaction of past and present releases the libido from the unconscious into the ego and in consequence increases ego-strength for creative coping. The interview (initial or other-wise) is therefore a testing ground for the patient's subse-quent action(s). The alternatives for such action are dis-cussed with the therapist, but the ultimate solution, outside the consulting room, will be that of the patient, and it will always be unique to him. Transference of course exists between patient and therapist, but as the patient becomes the observer of his own actions, feelings and thoughts, this feeling pattern is not used by the therapist through inter-pretation. The patient's emotional attention is not focused on the therapist but on those persons and situations of his life that cause him pain and pleasure. Because of the inter-action of the unconscious and the ego, and because psychic energy may be transformed through action(s) in the present, such significant or satisfying actions may alter the patient's image of himself and of others around him.

# 4 Using the Scale

*Faustus:* How comes it, then, that thou art out of hell?
*Mephistopheles:* Why, this is hell, nor am I out of it.*

In chapter 2 I described the various life areas that I studied
in connection with the satisfactions and frustrations of
patients, and I outlined the way in which a patient's responses
are scored, arriving at a maximum score of 100. I said that the
overall picture suggested that the ability to function adequately in society is related to the aggregate scores in the
five areas. What I have not said so far is that the scale **
is a treatment instrument which is given back to the patient
so that he can make some sense of what he has said. In treatment, therefore, the scale is not for the therapist but for
the patient; it is for *him* to review, for *him* to make sense of
and for *him* to act upon. The therapeutic use of the scale is
a more intensive method, used to assist the patient in the
creative process *after* the initial interview(s). The scale is
therefore an extension of the initial interview(s) and not
necessarily an alternative to it.

Before I devised the first scale in the 1950s, I had noticed
that one of the difficulties that people have is an inability to
make sense of our experiences, particularly when painful
situations are arising in our lives. There are often occasions
when life's experiences can be so overwhelming that we
truly do not know what goes on or where to start to sort
out the magnitude of problems that are pressing heavily on us.

I also noticed that when one can glance over answers given
at a certain point of time in regard to various areas of our
human existence, one can begin to make some order out of
the seeming chaos, and to sort out step by step the necessary
priorities. In a sense, therefore, we must be in a position to
take stock and to elaborate in a meaningful way on the
answers we have given to questions that are *our* questions.

---

* Marlowe, *The Tragical History of Doctor Faustus,* Act I.
** Throughout the book the HSSF — the Heimler Scale of Social Functioning —
will be referred to as 'the scale'.

The elaboration must be in some way stated, recorded, so that slowly, in the process of working through our problems, we find some way of understanding what it all adds up to. Often we are in no position to understand all, but at least we may understand something, and this something could be the first step in coping better with life, because we are able to rely on certain definite and tangible steps that we have been able to make.

Past and present are linked together by invisible wires and in a sense (as so many others have said), our todays reflect the problems and the solutions of our yesterdays. When we take stock with fifty-five questions before us, to which we give many more associations, we clarify at least something of the connections between past and present. Often such clarifications themselves have a therapeutic value, because we are perhaps in a position to see how the past has intruded into the present; by achieving some separation of these we may be able to deal with our present much more freely. Also it is quite possible that, without consciously taking notice of interfering elements from the past, some actions in the present may in fact pacify disturbing experiences in our yesterdays. For example, in a state of anxiety or panic, the really disturbing factors may have but little to do with the present, and if in any way we are capable of acting as adults, however minor this action may be, we may prove to ourselves that we are not helpless infants, and thus such separation between past and present can have (and often does have) freeing results.

In short, by our actions in the present we can send back messages through this invisible wire to our past, saying: 'This is now and that was then'. The observation of the answers given to fifty-five questions therefore helps in the process of separation, and paradoxically this may be the first step in the process of integration. As one patient said, 'I now realize I am not a helpless child, because I can act.' Such action is not defined necessarily as busily moving things about or rushing to do things. Quiet conversation with one's wife or friend or chief may be the beginning of further action. As the same patient said, 'I am also not helpless because I can talk.' Infants do not talk - they cannot!

And the action of talking separates the adult from the child, and through the *result* of such action we may integrate the child with the adult.

Before the scale is offered to the patient the therapist will explain to him very fully its motive, rationale and purpose. If I myself am giving this explanation, I will say to the patient: 'This scale came about because I was struggling, after very bitter experiences in my own life, to find some way of understanding the chaos that I had experienced in my past, and when I began to work with people like yourself I noticed that they too tried to find some meaning to what life is all about. I designed this scale not out of intellectual curiosity, nor simply to "help others", but in a sense also to help myself. I found it useful, and so did some others, and I hope you may benefit by it too.'

Whatever words are used, the important thing is to convey to the patient the message that the therapist himself has known a great deal of pain, and that the scale is not for examination or 'testing' but is an attempt to enable one to cope better with the human dilemma. It is important, I find, that the therapist conveys through his admission of his own struggles a sense of his humanity, and it is also important that I, the author who devised the scale, should appear not as a 'clever Dick' but as another suffering human being who understands, through personal experiences, that it is an integral part of life occasionally to face fear, anxiety, pain and conflict.

When I ask the question, for example, 'Do you like the work you are doing?' I have no way of knowing what the patient may have in mind. I simply cannot know what the word 'like' or the word 'work' may mean to him. The fact that I may or may not like my work has little or no relevance to the patient's liking his own work. I must notice, and I must not project my likes and dislikes on to the patient's likes and dislikes, nor must I think that he should or should not like his work just because I happen to do so or otherwise.

The meaning of the patient's answer can become clear at a later stage only, when he will tell me (and really tell himself) what 'like' and 'work' mean to *him*. Human experience is unique and individual, and each person has in mind highly individual and unique associations in regard to such questions as: 'Do you like the work you are doing?' It is quite likely that the same individual would give different answers to this question at other points in time. I do think that one of the secrets of human communication is to share the experiential meaning that lies behind words without judgement, approval or disapproval, but only with a great deal of understanding.

The patient has the right to know, before the scale is offered to him, what is the point of this exercise that he is to undertake. The therapist must be honest enough to tell him that its sole purpose is to enable the patient to reflect upon his life, because this is sometimes very difficult to do without some kind of framework or 'container'. Sometimes, as I said before, life can be so overbearing that we need some container within which we can examine at least something about our lives.

I usually introduce the actual questions and the answers that will be given by the patient with something like this:

I shall now ask you a number of questions, and it will only take a few minutes to go through this list. Please answer: 'Yes', 'Perhaps', or 'No', according to how you *feel* about the questions *now*. If you are uncertain about some answers, or if you feel that 'sometimes' would apply, your answer no doubt would be 'Perhaps'. If you feel that you don't know some of the answers, or if you feel that you are unsure, but that you simply don't know, let me know. We cannot score this latter. Please answer me as you feel, and make an immediate response to my questions. If by any chance later you wish to change any of your answers, you will have the opportunity to do so. As the whole idea of the scale is to have it later to study your reactions to your answers, please do not comment on anything while I am asking the questions. Whatever *you* understand by the question is what you should answer. I will now put the questions to you, so please answer me 'Yes', 'Perhaps', 'No', as you feel.

In order to give some idea of the questions in the scale, here is an example of one question from each section:

| | |
|---|---|
| Section 1 (work): | Do you like the work you are doing? |
| Section 2 (financial): | Do you live more comfortably |

|  |  |
|---|---|
| | than you did two years ago? |
| Section 3 (friendship): | Have you a close friend in whom you can confide? |
| Section 4 (family): | Do you feel that your partner (husband/wife) understands you? |
| Section 5 (personal): | Does sex bring you much enjoyment in your marriage? |
| from Section 1 (work) on the negative (or frustration) index: | Do you feel overworked? |
| from Section 2 (finance) on the negative index: | Is your imagination painful to you? |
| from Section 3 (friendship) on the negative index: | Would you like to have more power and influence? |
| from Section 4 (family) on the negative index: | Are you at times very depressed? |
| from Section 5 on the negative index: | Are you inclined to drink too much? |
| finally a question (out of five) from the synthesis index: | Do you feel that your life has meaning? |

After fifty-five questions have been asked and answered, I often invite the patient to dictate to me his scored responses, which I then transfer to the front page of the scale; or I may ask him to fill in his own form. While dictating his responses to me the patient is in fact taking the lead because I have to rely on the information that he gives me. This often adds to the patient's feeling of self-effectiveness.

| SCALE | TOTALS<br>T(4s) / T(4 + 2s) | MEAN<br>TOTAL |
|---|---|---|
| POSITIVE | 76/88 | 82 |
| NEGATIVE | 12/22 | 17 |
| SYNTHESIS | – | 82 |

| POSITIVE INDEX | | | | | | | | NEGATIVE INDEX | | | | | | | SYNTHESIS |
|---|---|---|---|---|---|---|---|---|---|---|---|---|---|---|---|
| Area | Part | 1 | 2 | 3 | 4 | 5 | Totals | Area | 1 | 2 | 3 | 4 | 5 | Totals | |
| work | A | 4 | 2 | 4 | 2 | 4 | 12/16 | activity | 0 | 0 | 0 | 2 | 0 | 0/2 | 1) 18 |
| | – | – | – | – | – | – | – | somatic | 0 | 2 | 0 | 0 | 0 | 0/4 | 2) 16 |
| finance | A | 4 | 4 | 4 | 4 | 2 | 16/18 | persecution | 0 | 0 | 2 | 0 | 4 | 4/6 | 3) 18 |
| friendship | | 4 | 4 | 2 | 4 | 4 | 16/18 | depression | 0 | 2 | 0 | 0 | 0 | 0/2 | 4) 16 |
| family | A | | | | | | | escape routes | 0 | 4 | 0 | 4 | 0 | 8/8 | 5) 14 |
| | B | 2 | 4 | 4 | 4 | 4 | 16/18 | | | | | | | | |
| personal | A | 4 | 4 | 4 | 2 | 4 | 16/18 | | | | | | | | |
| | | | | Totals: | | | 76/88 | | | | | | Totals: | 12/22 | 82 |

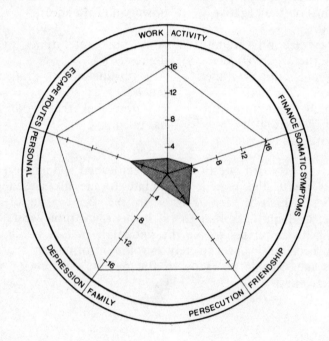

Diagram of a forty-six-year-old professional man who functions very well. The straight lines indicate the perimeter of the satisfaction area; the shaded area frustration.

The graphic illustration of the satisfaction-frustration pattern is represented by two circles equally divided into five sections (see figure). On the right-hand side of each section appears one of the five areas of satisfaction, and on the left each of the five areas of frustration. The radius shows appropriate score totals in each of the respective areas. This graphic illustration is presented to the patient only if there is either a balance between satisfaction and frustration or if satisfaction overwhelms frustration. This pictorial presentation of the two relationships can have, and usually does have, a considerable impact on the patient. The shading of the frustration area allows the patient to see at a glance his present-day life situation. If frustration dominates present life experiences, and consequently the shaded area encircles the outlined area, the sudden impact of perception may cause some shock to some patients. In such a case the graphic presentation is delayed until the patient's further responses have been obtained or, as stated earlier, it may be avoided altogether. This graphic presentation (devised by Miss J. L. Dighton) gives only a feel of the satisfaction-frustration relationship, and has no scientific basis. The pairing of areas (positive and negative) is entirely arbitrary, and different patterns of pairing would bring about a totally different spacial image. Although there may be some connection between friendship and persecution areas, or between work and paralysis of activity, the graphic presentation aims to bring about feeling responses only, and it may be an additional help in the process of self-observation. In a sense, the circle represents life experiences that contain both positive and negative features.

I always explain to the patient that it is very important that he gives 'yes', 'perhaps' or 'no' answers to the questions, and that having given such answers he can then tell me what these answers *mean* to him. It usually takes a little time before the patient makes a start on his reflection. He may ask me for still more clarification on some issues that are not quite clear to him. He may need help with the process of 'ignition'; but once he begins he usually has little difficulty in proceeding with his own interpretation.

Some patients may comment on what now appear to be contradictory statements; some will make use of the opportunity to expand on what they had meant by this and that. The amount of information forthcoming will in any case be greater than is obtained through a more usual type of interview. For example, to the question, 'Do you feel overworked?' one patient associated overwork with a feeling of pressure, which did not come from outside but from within. 'As soon as I get down to it, I feel sweaty, and have an unpleasant feeling in the pit of my stomach. I can't talk myself out of it. It just comes on me.' He explained that this occurred particularly when he had to do something that he was reluctant to do. In an ordinary interview, a patient would not have the same opportunity of self-observation.

From time to time I help the patient by summing up what he has said, and he can stop and think about my summaries.

We use words, sentences, thoughts and feelings to express what we wish to communicate, and through this expression we try to convey ourselves to others. But seldom do we have the opportunity to convey ourselves to ourselves in a systematic way. Our lives contain many unformulated questions that never have a chance to be formulated, and there are many unformulated answers that can seldom be collected into meaningful units. Human beings, so it seems, often use communication with others in order to try to formulate such questions and answers. The 'other', then, is being used as a mirror that will reflect one's own experiences. If two people do this simultaneously, then there is little communication between the two, as each attempts to use the other for his own questions and answers. As most questions and answers float within us with some diffusion and confusion, we have but seldom the opportunity to separate questions and answers. We may very well be afraid of the answers when only the questions are frightening, or we may be afraid of the questions when the answers seem to be threatening. Sometimes communication with others becomes a testing ground for our muddled thinking. In such a situation the 'other' becomes the object of our likes and dislikes according to what is reflected back to us by the 'mirror'. How can we hope to listen, to understand, and truly to co-operate with others when most of the time we are incapable of separating our own questions from our own answers, and other people's questions and answers from our own? How can we learn to separate our own experiences from those of others?

I believe that the scale offers some solution to this process of separation and self-observation. The solution is by no means perfect, but it could be, and often is, the beginning of a way towards a better level of overall functioning. What has previously been experienced as internal is now reflected upon and so becomes externalized onto the scale; a rough map lies in front of the patient. I notice that this process of self-observation usually brings about some clarification of problems, or at least a different way of perceiving them, and also some recognition of the way in which life patterns are interconnected (for example, someone may do a great deal of overtime, rationalizing that this is for financial reasons only, and he may now see connections between this and some difficulty in the family or marriage relationship).

I also notice that the ability to ask relevant questions and the attempt to formulate some answers to such questions is very helpful in separating oneself from a feeling of inadequacy and often regressed behaviour, particularly when as a result of this there appears an urge to do something about one's predicament.

Having done this work for many years, it seems to me that as life's experiences are being observed in a disciplined way a great deal of psychic energy is freed that was eagerly awaiting a productive or creative release. Self-observation cannot usually define the direction of that potential release: this will come much later in the therapeutic process.

Recording and playing back is, I think, an important part of this method, and I have already mentioned this in connection with the initial interview. Whether I play back everything the patient states as he reviews his answers on the scale, or only part of it, or none at all, depends on a great many considerations, the most important being the patient's own reactions to such a procedure. As the process of reflection takes place the patient (or I, on behalf of the patient) will record in writing or on a tape-recorder summaries, which will consist of questions, statements, or simply capsulations of what has been said. The process here is also similar to the one I described in the initial interview.

The patient whom I quoted earlier on page 52 as having 'self-pressurizing', sweating and stomach pains listened to the playback on the tape-recorder of all that he had said, then asked: 'But . . . isn't the question really that I do things that I dislike? Now, do I need to do them? Do I have an alternative?' Later he summed up: 'Really, the question is not the discomfort, but the nature of the job itself. I must do something about that.'

As I completed many of these interviews I came to the tentative conclusion that human experience can be reviewed very positively if we understand that it has a purpose. If we can understand not only that life can be made meaningful but that life wants to be meaningful, then there is optimism and hope. The search for a theme or a meaning or simply a recognition of what it all adds up to is therefore 'goal-directed' not because I wish it to be so, but because everything that I have experienced in my own life so far has proved to me that man's existence without personal meaning makes him feel at odds with himself and others.

The search for a theme or themes does not come naturally; it comes only by seeking, and often through very great personal pain. I do not want to give the impression it happens always, or happens easily. But when it happens (and often it does), then realization comes to the patient that his pain has some purpose and in a sense was his guide. Once this knowledge comes through, he will be less afraid of life and its problems.

But what are we to do with the tension that comes through this process when one feels that something ought to be done? I think the clarification of intention is the channelling of tension. I must not delude myself that great changes will occur in my consulting-room. Release through action belongs to life as it is lived outside the consulting-room. 'Channelling' means that possible alternatives and their repercussions and perhaps implications are aired so that the patient may

choose satisfying rather than frustrating solutions. Ultimately, however, it will be he who will make the choice and
the subsequent actions in his life. I can discuss with him
the spectrum of choices but I have no way of knowing what
colour or colours he will actually choose. I believe, however (and only very occasionally do I find it otherwise),
that it is valid to trust that a patient, when he knows what
the choices are, will choose the right one for himself.

A married woman patient reviewed her situation with her
husband in an interview with me. He had been having an
affair with his colleague, a single middle-aged woman. My
patient knew about this relationship but for obscure reasons
felt that her husband was entitled to his affair, because she
herself 'could not give him what he needed'. Just before
she came to see me, however, the situation changed. Her
husband now spent more and more time with his mistress,
yet 'at all costs' (as he put it to his wife) wanted to remain
with his wife under the same roof. In fact he wanted both
women. The patient carefully examined the many and varied
aspects of her married life and of her own personal needs
until she felt that two possibilities were open to her: either
to remain in the situation she was in and deny herself the
right to be *someone,* or to bring the marriage to an end and
live alone, building a new life for herself, despite her age.
The interview clarified her problems. She decided to leave.

Finally, apart from giving the patient further opportunity in subsequent interviews to explore his actions and
ultimately to choose those that may have a lasting effect
on his life, I may, towards a terminating session, once more
work through the scale with the patient, so that we can
both observe the changes in his responses. This may help
him to evaluate changes that have occurred and to see more
precisely the journey he has undertaken, the solution that
he has sought and the problems that he has not yet solved.

Using the scale as part of the treatment of individuals
naturally often leads to treatment of the family as a whole.
This will be described in a later chapter.

*Treatment session with 'Betty' (case 2)*
(Age 31, single, teacher)

Only Betty's reaction and observation of her scale scores will be recorded here for demonstration purposes. She has had an initial interview. The following is taken from the second interview with Betty, which was tape-recorded. The only alterations are minor stylistic changes to help the reader to go through the process with as much clarity as possible. Some references by Betty to the initial interview have also been omitted. Finally, this long interview has had to be shortened for practical purposes, but the essential features appear as Betty stated them.

*Betty* I seem to have very little satisfaction in my work.

(Long silence)

*Therapist* Would you write this down please.

*Betty* I have little work satisfaction . . . due to circumstances.

(She writes this down)

In the light of what I have just said, I would like to change the answer I gave you to question two: 'On the whole, do you like the people you work with?' I said 'perhaps'. Now that I think of it, the answer may be, or should be, 'yes'. A lot of it is me too, it's not just my colleagues. I am able, so far, to refuse to let people's attitudes towards me affect my attitude towards them. There is a younger colleague. I very much feel at times with her when someone — and it often happens — kind of steps on her toes. At times I would take this very personally and react to it, as if it happened to me. However, this feeling is changing now. I can . . . I try to be less involved . . .

*Therapist* Could you summarize what you have just said?

*Betty* (After a very long pause, writes, then reads:)

I am able, so far in my work situation, to refuse to react to resistance I feel in others, so that their resistance has nothing to feed on . . . you know this brings something into my mind. There was this Negro fellow who worked next door . . . [laughs] . . . I was scared . . . so I refused to have a drink with him . . . [laughs] . . . all right, let me look now at the financial section . . . that may change. The friendship area is the one that keeps me going.

*Therapist* You say that it is this area that keeps you going?

*Betty* It has to be so. What else *could* really?

(She reads aloud the questions and her responses in the friendship area.)

Now, how would I summarize this section? Something here does not fit. If I don't trust people how can I really feel that I have people in whom I can confide, or think that there are people who really care for me?

(Writes, and reads:)

If I don't trust myself and others, how can I have a close friend in whom I can confide, and how can I expect that there are people who really care?

*Therapist* What does this question of yours really mean to you? Could you explain?

*Betty* There are some people I do trust.

*Therapist* Could you put that down on paper too?

*Betty* (Writes, then says:)

The thing I keep thinking about is, that it's not because of me that I trust some people, but because of . . . Man . . . maybe I trust myself too a little bit.

(She writes this down).

I haven't really thought of this before . . . but it may be that because I really do trust myself . . . [very long silence] . . . all right . . . there are only two people [names them] whom I really trust. Why do I trust them? And why do I trust myself with the two of them? [Both those named are men.] Maybe, because . . . I know that both of them have basically the same religious conviction as I have. Both of them have a strength of character to carry out their convictions. I wonder . . . if I have that kind of strength too? Maybe I am not sure that I have. Maybe that I . . . have . . .

*Therapist* Could I sum up my understanding of what you have told me? Have you in fact said: 'I, Betty, have some strength of character, religious conviction, and I have the ability to follow through on these; and I trust those in whom I see the same'?

*Betty* No, I am not saying that. Maybe what I am saying is . . . that I want to have these things but I am not sure that I have them unless I am with others who do have them.

(Writes this down.)

*Therapist* Now let's go through your summaries and see if some theme or themes that you see may emerge, something that might help you to do something about what you have said so far.

*Betty* (She reads from her notes:)

If I don't trust myself and others, how can I have a close friend in whom I can confide, and how can I expect that there are people who really care?

(She now reads the rest of her summaries quietly, here and there emphasizing a word or two aloud.)

What frightens me, as I look at this [the summaries] is the feeling that I am capable of being the exact opposite of what I want to be, or wish to be . . .

(Very long silence, while she is reflecting on her summaries.)

It seems to add up to this: I am really very unsure of myself.

*Therapist* Is that the message that you get out of your summaries?

*Betty* The message is really my need to become more sure of myself, but . . . I have to get to the point when I have to overcome the paralysis, the feeling of rejection and being, or feeling, rejected. [Pause] It's really centred round some lack of acceptance, but I don't want to be just accepted.

*Therapist* Will you put this down - 'I don't want to be just accepted'.

*Betty* (Writes it down.)

I would like to add that I *will* not be *just* accepted. It's ridiculous but it's true.

*Therapist* What seems ridiculous?

*Betty* I will not be just accepted, I want to be something special! [laughs] Now listen to this: I will not be just accepted, I will be something special, and this will include all my 'wants'. That's it.

*Therapist* All right. We shall meet again next week.

## Treatment sessions with 'Harry' (case 3)
(Age 25, single, kitchen porter)
In the previous case ('Betty') I have attempted to describe the *process* of scale interview in treatment. In this case I shall describe Harry's dilemma, and his ultimate solution, without describing details of the process of treatment. Harry's case covers a period of seven months of interviews and scale sessions. He is now (in 1973) thirty-four years old and the interviews took place in 1964-5. This case is descriptive of the scale method; it will attempt to give a retrospective picture of treatment, since 'Harry' and I have had the opportunity of meeting since the case was closed in April 1965. In order to reconstruct this case I have used my original notes, together with Harry's notes and one tape-recorded session. I have also relied on my own memory.

### The Duke
Big cities are lonely places for those who are alone, but none is more lonely than London. Although new buildings periodically replace old ones, something of the past is being locked up in vast tenement houses as well as in the mansions of those who had separated themselves from the mass. The often grey sky seems to emphasize the drab greyness of the streets, and the rain only adds to an atmosphere of hopelessness. At least, this was Harry's perception of the capital city when he arrived from Ireland to seek a better life.

He came to the big city from a small village near the Atlantic Ocean, from a farming family that could not keep up with expenses. The farm had died a slow death - it certainly could not support Harry or several of his brothers. The family broke up following the death of Harry's mother. The 'old man' remained on the farm, slowly dying with it. In 1959 Harry packed his bag and came to London. His only real possession was a golden cross which he wore around his neck, a present from mother on his ninth birthday. When he sold that cross one Saturday morning in south London, when for days, penniless, he had walked the endless streets, he felt that his past had slipped away from him. He felt that it was not any longer *his* past and that he was living in a vacuum without past or future. After selling the cross he bought himself a cup of tea, ate a large plateful of sausages and eggs, and went to a nearby church. Did the good Lord hear his cries?

The city was like a polyp, the streets like hundreds of arms suffocating him. Sometimes he worked in the building trade, sometimes he was on National Assistance. The polyp's arms were not paved with gold. He lived in 'digs' in Bermondsey, south London. When he could not pay the rent, he moved on. He drifted from job to job, from digs to digs, and he felt that life was slipping away from him.

Harry had his dreams: a dark-haired girl with green eyes waiting for him in a modern block of flats. The bedroom was warm and his naked wife offered him all the pleasures of the world. As he lay sleepless in one or other of his bare rooms in Bermondsey he saw that vision so very clearly that at times he would reach out for her . . . He had other dreams too. When he was a child, a few miles away was the mansion of a Duke, a rich man with many servants, well respected, who spent most of his time in London, where he sat at the House of Lords, or travelling around the world. To Harry, in his dreary existence, the Duke had become everything that he himself was not. He did not know how and when it happened, but one night he saw himself as the Duke, and His Grace was speaking to him from a far corner of the room, further away than the reality of the walls would permit. The Duke was powerful; he 'owned' the brunette with green eyes; he wildly made love to her and she, the perfect mistress, responded to the Duke's embraces. Sometimes he would wake from heavy sleep to hear the Duke abusing him. Yes - 'Harry the Duke' was hearing 'Harry the nothing' answering. He became frightened because the Duke told him to kill himself.

It was the priest who first noticed Harry's mental illness.

'You must seek help, my son. You need help now.'

But Harry was unwilling to say farewell to the Duke.

'Father, he is my only friend, I have no friends.'

As the months and the years went by, the Duke spoke to him not only in the stillness of the night but also during the day. He spoke to him while he was working as a kitchen porter in a big all-night restaurant. On the occasions when he applied for his National Assistance 'Harry the nothing' slowly gave way to 'Harry the Duke' until he became almost the Duke himself.

Then Father Patrick took a strong line, took 'Harry the Duke' by the hand, and the doctor at the clinic gave him a new fancy title which he in due course learned: schizophrenia.

Although according to the law Harry was ill, he could not be forced to enter a mental hospital. 'Harry the Duke' did not want to go. He agreed, however, to be seen by the local authority mental health department. And so one day he appeared on my doorstep.

### The Duke gives way

Before Harry's appearance at my office in Westminster I too had gone through a grave crisis. During the spring a tumour had been removed from my back, a tumour that turned out to be malignant. If it had not been for the insistence of my wife that I should seek medical advice on what I had considered to be a little 'pimple', it is unlikely that I would now be writing this book, or indeed that I should ever have met Harry. After the operation I was frankly told that I had had a very unusual form of skin cancer and that it would be some years before we would know for certain whether there would be a recurrence or a spreading of the disease. My own diagnosis was impressive too: dermato-fibro-sarcoma pretruberans. I was forty-two years old at the time, struggling with the concepts and methods of social functioning, married with two small children; and it seemed to me that I might never be able to finish, either as father or as professional man, what I had started, what I had aimed for. I knew that I should have to live for some years in 'the shadow of death', and I eventually made up my mind to try to make the best job of it. This decision, however, did not come about through my adopting a stiff-upper-lip attitude; it was the result of a great deal of heart-searching about life, about living and about dying. For the second time I had had to face death, and on this occasion the penny dropped with a louder clang.

The relevance of these experiences of mine to the case of 'Harry' is this: that I decided amongst other things to go ahead in my own way and to do the things that hitherto I had hesitated to do. When one knows that death may be around the corner it is sometimes easier to free oneself more from convention and to deviate from the beaten track.

As I listened to Harry's story about the Duke I could not help asking myself, who was this Duke? Could he represent that part of Harry that could never find expression in reality? Did the presence of the

Duke not indicate that there was a part of Harry that contained all those powers, but that, in his present predicament and through lack of knowledge of himself, he had projected all these feelings outside himself? If Harry could find in *outer reality* the powers he gave to the Duke, would the Duke not disappear from Harry's life? Had I not learned enough about psychic energy to know that if this energy is not externalized it is bound to move into 'internal immigration'?

I considered it my first task to explore Harry's ability or abilities, all those aspects of his libido that up to the present he did not, or could not, use. In short, I took note of the Duke and then proceeded to use him in Harry's real life. The 'Duke' to me was indeed Harry's only friend, but alas! not in the way that Harry had perceived him. *The Duke became destructive only because his reality was not acknowledged and used by Harry.*

As I thought that I might have but little time, I did everything I could in as short a time as possible to help Harry to externalize his psychic energies.

First, with the help of a psychologist, we established Harry's IQ. This was certainly well above the level of his actual performance.

Secondly, it was clear to me that without some educational achievement Harry had no chance to actualize the Duke. Although my patient's concentration was somewhat impaired, I used my session with him (once, twice, sometimes three times a week) to assist him to prepare for his O levels.

My 'treatment' sessions with Harry involved my teaching him subjects I had long forgotten. I relearned with him history, mathematics, English and the rest. In a relatively short space of time he managed to pass in two subjects. By that time his interest began to expand and he saw that with further learning he could make something of his life. He had considerable, but never recognized, artistic ability; he had long forgotten how well he used to be able to draw when at school.

Now, as he reflected on his life, on his scale responses, on what he had and on what he had not, the ambition of making something of himself became very apparent. Within eight months the Duke had given way to 'Harry the something'.

I was able to secure a grant for him, and long after he had stopped seeing me professionally he went to art school. At the time of writing he is a commercial artist. He has found friends, male and female, and London now is not such a frightening and lonely place as it was when he arrived. Harry, having found his niche, and being able to put his inner psychic energies to use, has no further need for the Duke. He told me some months ago that he has had a chance to travel a little and the world that he used to dream about has become outwardly explorable for him.

Throughout the interviews with Harry, little was said about his past and a great deal about his present and future. Little was said about the 'why' of his problem, but more concentration was put on the 'what' and the 'how'. Even his other title, schizophrenia, is now of little relevance. He is moving in life, and thus life can move within him.

Finally, I learned that Harry had married and had a son.

## Summary notes on the scale

The scale as a treatment tool is primarily for the use of the patient. Through the statement of satisfaction and frustration, he may reflect on answers given and on the relationships between such answers. It allows the patient to look at his life at a given time, to associate to it, to his past, to separate his past from his present and eventually through action to integrate the two once more.

The use of the scale as a treatment tool can be made only through a truly peer-relationship with the patient; by channelling the patient's libido and wish for transference-relationship away from the therapist and towards persons and objectives *outside* the consulting-room; by skilful and disciplined methodology to help the patient to become the observer of his life-situation with a view to subsequent action and increasingly freed psychic energy, so that he may move towards satisfying goals by thorough examination of possible alternative actions. The therapist may concentrate on very defined action to be carried out by the patient (with Harry it was some educational achievement); and my experience and knowledge has taught me that such actions do not confine themselves to limited areas but rather open up satisfactions in other life areas. It appears to me that the therapist may have to play many roles (in Harry's case I had to become his teacher).

Finally, the use of the scale in treatment may help to increase ego strength. I suppose that is what the whole process I have described is all about.

# 5 The Statement

The fragmenta vitae (slice of life), referred to here as the statement, is a further treatment method that I have found very useful in short-term dealings with patients.

The statement is an exploration of a limited time period (about fifteen to twenty-five minutes) of the last twenty-four hours before the interview. The patient may choose any such period during that time sequence, and is asked to relate as much as he can recall as he experienced it. The time spent by the patient in this recall of experiences from the near past will, of course, vary from individual to individual. The actual recollection of experience in the present has little bearing on the actual time experience of the near-past period.

The patient's entire statement is recorded on tape and then played back to him. During playback he is asked to stop the tape recorder at any time when any thought, reaction, or observation *presents itself for communication* with and to the therapist. Such interruptions, however irrelevant they may seem, are separately recorded on a sheet of paper by the patient, and such comments as he makes will be his 'material' from which he may build his future action(s). As the totality of his comments will be recognized by him to be all relevant to his life situation, such totality contains a message or a theme that will guide him into meaningful action outside the consulting-room.

## Rationale

I have said earlier that an experience will have meaning only if I am capable of observing that which happens to me, that which I feel. As experiences passing through time do not yield themselves for observation, life appears as a series of unconnected and meaningless happenings; our yesterdays having been denied, we have no access to the moment of the day and always desperately seek for a better chance tomorrow. It is not really surprising that tomorrow has the same fate as today, and we move across our fading years with an increasing feeling of emptiness.

Hardly anywhere have we now the chance to be alone with our *own* experiences. People on the whole are not able to listen to others, as they have not learned how to listen to themselves. There is a desperate and urgent need to communicate, but as no one is listening, we are living in an age of 'verbal diarrhoea'; the more we say, the less understood we feel. Even some psychotherapists do not listen. They take in certain amounts of information in order to interpret to their patients the result of *their* conclusions. As a patient I can hardly be alone with my own experiences, if I know that such experiences are listened to by my therapist from a particular point of view, and for a particular reason.

While we pay lip-service to the patient's right to self-determination, we have lost our respect for him, and do not believe that he can determine his own life-route. If we cannot use our own experiences (say the therapists) how can we believe that the client can use his? Denial of experience then gives way to professional dogma, technique, and the intellectual conviction that *we* hold some key for *him*. But no man holds the key to another man's lock; each man has to find alone his own key that will fit into his own lock. In order that he may find it, he has to be trusted, to be believed capable, and to be offered a framework within which he can be alone with his present and his past. *The primary role of the therapist is to help the patient to find a solid framework in which to decipher the unique meaning of his life-experiences.* The statement is such a framework.

The statement process consists of the following interconnected phases:

1) statement by the patient of a fifteen to twenty-five minute 'slice' of his last twenty-four hours;

2) simultaneous tape-recording of same;

3) patient listens to the recording, writing down summaries of his/her reactions to it;

4) search by the patient for a theme (or themes) running through the summaries;

5) discussion between patient and therapist as to possible

future action, implications, etc;
6) sometimes (as in the following case-study), the use of
the time-interaction technique.
Such methods have great similarity to the dialogue (see
chapter 6).

*Interview with 'Tom' (case 4)*
(Age 36, married, 3 children, draughtsman)
Tom contacted me while I was in the United States, in connection, as he said, with a specific problem. This concerned
his feelings towards his wife, and particularly her attitude
towards his three small children.
The following is a reconstruction from the actual tape-
recording of the interview.

*E. H.* All right. Now just tell me anything you see and experience
in relation to your wife during yesterday.

(The reader is reminded that in the statement a limited time period
out of the last twenty-four hours is chosen *by the patient*.)

The whole thing will not take longer than fifteen minutes.

*Tom* I am sitting in the big red chair in my living-room at my chosen
point of time and I am reading the newspaper, while Kay my wife is
at the bottom of the stairs yelling at the kids to clear up the rooms.
The two kids are upstairs and the baby is in the bedroom. The kids
upstairs are playing around and not listening to their mother, so she
is screaming more at them and threatening them.

*E. H.* What is she saying?

(The statement is presented not in past but in present tense as if the
action were to take place *in the present*.)

*Tom* If they do not listen to her she will come up in five minutes and
beat them. The children don't take any notice of her and then she runs
upstairs and keeps screaming at them. I am sitting in the living-room and
getting more and more angry and thinking how useless and ineffective
this handling of hers of the children is. I feel, why isn't she *doing* something about the kids instead of just screaming at them? However, I
myself don't do anything. I don't do anything because I feel she will
only get madder if I say anything to her and that wouldn't help. It

also occurs to me while I am reading the paper that I could go up and help the kids and control them; but I reject that because I would have to do something which I think is really more her job. So I don't do anything. I just sit. She doesn't know about how I feel. She doesn't even notice me while all this is going on. I am feeling very hateful towards her, really feeling like hitting her or screaming also. Inside me I am really screaming at her, but I don't say anything. I am beginning to feel immobilized; just trapped, stuck.

*E.H.* Come back to this time and place for a minute. Put yourself at the age of sixty and try to visualize where you would be; the location and the time - morning, afternoon or evening. Remember that you are an older man. Have you got an image?

*Tom* Yes. (Uncertain)
Can I choose anywhere? Can I choose being surrounded by nature?

*E.H.* Yes. Anything. Wherever you are now, and you have that fixed in your mind, your present self aged thirty-six is now approaching that older self of sixty and asking him how you did manage to overcome this difficulty with your wife.

(Silence)

What I am asking you to do is to allow your young self, facing your old self, to reflect on how the old man has solved this problem.

(Silence)

*Tom* I did it by finally doing something. One day I went after my wife, when she was screaming, and I said: 'Come with me'. We went to the bedroom and I talked to her very calmly, although I had many emotions; and I told her that too. I told her that we must talk about this, because the way it is going is not helpful and it is not helping anybody; her or me or the kids; and we have to find in our lives some different ways, different ways with each other and different ways with the kids. I felt that by talking about it I was more helpful than by just doing nothing. I also felt that this interchange between us was more helpful than her hitting the kids. I told her that whether she wants to talk about it or not, we are going to do so. I shared with her my decision that I have resolved that this is where we have to start; talking. Once we started speaking to each other about our problems with the children (and that was not too easy because we were getting on to the usual side-roads, but we still stuck to it) then we got into all kinds of other things besides the kids. So that opened up many many things. There were tears and a lot of different kinds of feelings; good feelings, bad feelings. This kind of opening up between us went on for many years. That was the start then. Eventually we had reached an agreement with each other so that when things are getting out of hand we would have a contract to sit down and start talking about our differences and our problems. So our talking to each other ended up in our doing things differently eventually. In the end there was much more give and take as we have shared more together. So across the years we kind of worked things out; many problems came up, but it seemed more easy to cope with them better. There was anger and there was resentment. There was love but we did not stop doing this. So in the end we kind of worked it out.

*E.H.* Once more I ask you to come back to this time and place here with me, and finally I would like to ask you to choose a particular memory when you were a small child, any age, particularly between the ages of five or six or seven years, if you can still remember and try to see an actual memory. If it is difficult for you to go as far back, then any time in your childhood will be fine. Choose one event and tell me where you are, what you are doing. Can you see yourself as a child? Where are you? How old are you?

*Tom* What I am looking at now is kind of random. I am about ten I would guess. I am with one of my friends and we are standing at the edge of the road in New York City. I have a slingshot and the car is coming up the hill and I place a rock into the slingshot and let go and shoot. I wasn't meaning to hit the car. I was just trying to see how close I could aim without hitting it. Anyway, the rock hit the ground, bounced, and hit the car. I got very scared. By that time my dad came out of the house and was quite angry with me. He told me to get into the house and sent my friend home, I went into my sister's bedroom and stood by the closed closet. I might even have hid myself inside the closet. My dad came back after talking to the driver. He just gave me one swipe. I don't really remember that it really hurt but I was very frightened about the whole thing.

*E.H.* All right. Leave it there. Now you are left alone. Your father had left the room. And now you at the age of thirty-six years enter. I would like you to have a little conversation with the child and find out if he ever thought that he would get married one day and whether this is the way that you have imagined it as it is. Ask the child whether this is in fact what you wanted. Or whether what he wanted - whichever way you look at it.

*Tom* So am I telling him about my present self?

*E.H.* Yes, and see what he says.

*Tom* As a child I did imagine that I would get married one day and have children, but this is not the way I imagined that it would be. Frankly I don't have a very clear picture of what it would be, except a lot of happiness, things which I have seen in the movies and what children are supposed to think at that age about marriage - that it would be nice to have somebody around and nice to share your life with somebody, to have breakfast with her. A lot of my life as a child was rather lonely. Now at the age of thirty-six I found that you can have an equally lonely life although you have a wife around. Sometimes even more so. So at this point aged thirty-six it hasn't really worked out the way I wanted it to and I get pretty discouraged whether it ever is going to work out. Every now and then I see a little bit of a glimmer of hope that perhaps it will be something that I wanted but I don't really think that it ever will be what I have imagined it to be. That dream would be kind of unrealistic. However, I think things can be improved. But it sure takes a lot of work.

*E.H.* Let's stop it there. I shall wind back the tape and you can listen. As you are listening to what you have said so far you can stop the tape recorder at any point whenever and wherever you feel that any thought and idea occurs to you. I would like you to write down any such reactions whatever they may be on this piece of paper and then we shall see at the end what we have got.

(The above, then, was played back to Tom and he did in fact stop the tape-recorder several times and at the end he wrote down the following as he was listening to the whole session replayed to him.)

*Tom* (Reading out his reactions to listening to the recording:)

My relationship with my wife is not very satisfying.
   1) The actions and the feelings between my wife and me are not very satisfying.
   2) My wife screaming at the kids - I feel very angry but I don't

know what to do about it.

3) I am angry because she does things I don't want her to do, and I feel like a kid she is screaming at. I am caught between good and bad and end up being helpless.

4) I feel like I am boiling inside when I am angry and I feel like being violent.

5) I feel like a kid with my wife and I don't like it.

6) What do I have to do to be a man with my wife?

(As he reflected on his answers the main theme that had emerged that was significant to him was his reference to what he has to do to be a man with his wife.)

*Tom* (Reaction) I get upset when I see illogical things being done by my wife. I ought to do something but I don't do anything. I tell Kay to do something but I don't do anything. My fears of feeling like a kid; feeling weak and helpless and not doing things that I feel would be helpful. My wife's screaming stirs up many feelings of helplessness and the feeling of wanting to hit back.

I feel closer to my wife because we are doing something together.

(This is at the point of tape when he in retrospect talks to himself at age thirty-six from age sixty.)

Together means not being in opposition to joining ourselves in action and feeling. I feel this way when I heard myself talking with her about our problems. I like the sound of me being firm and saying this is what we are going to do. My main feeling about my dad was fear. I got angry with my dad because he unjustly accused me; I could not explain.

(This is a reference to the rock-throwing incident.)

I didn't know what marriage would be like because my parents were divorced when I was two. I frequently feel very alone when I am with my wife. I am not sure what I can have and what I can't have.

*E.H.* Now think about what you have written down there as you were listening to the tape. Tell me when you have got it what it all adds up to, whether there is some kind of a message there for you.

*Tom* The theme that has been running through in many ways — being helpless on the one side and doing something, talking, some action, on the other side. Power and weakness. One answer seems to be that the only thing so far in the way of doing is to talk.

(Silence)

When I think about that my head says 'that is doing' but the rest of me is not that hot about the idea. I would rather do something more besides just talking, but I don't know what that [doing] is.

Maybe talking is the beginning and as we are talking other things will come; more powerful things, and more action.

(Silence)

Which means I might have to be kind of . . . I can't get everything I want right now, but I have gradually to work towards it. I can't do all the action right now. With my wife we have to do some talking first, and then maybe I can get some action later.

*E.H.* All right. We have summed up what is there. What will it be then?

(Silence while he is studying his notes that he has taken during the recording)

*Tom* Well. I am not really helpless because we can talk and talk can lead to some action.

(Long silence)

*E.H.* All right. Are you satisfied with this answer? With the final summary of what you have said?

*Tom* Yes. In one way. Although — I mean yes, it tells me the answer but it may not be as dramatic as my guts would like it to be. It seems that I am very impatient for something more dramatic, as if something would change the world today. That is going to take a little while but that is more solid.

*E.H.* Earlier you have put a question to yourself: 'What have I got to do to be a man with my wife?' Have you found an answer to that?

*Tom* I said earlier that I am not helpless because I can do things that will lead to some action; this is too vague, 'doing things'. I am not helpless because I can take my action. I like that. Because there is more to it than talking.

Tom has problems with his wife, because of her mishandling

of their children. He does not know how to cope with these problems and how to deal with his anger. Instead of telling me in descriptive terms what bothers him (i.e., 'evenings are always full of tension because my wife screams at the children and I cannot, or do not, do anything, but I feel an impotent anger within me'), I ask him to choose a significant event (i.e. significant to him) from his experiences of the last twenty-four hours. He defines the actual time by saying, for example, 'It was about 6.30 last night, after I had returned from work.' I am asking him to present to me (and to himself, of course) the events following, say between 6.30 and 7 pm, not in a descriptive way, but rather *as if he were experiencing last night's happenings now.* After some reflection, he places himself *into* that time and begins to recall events as if they were taking place now, during the interview. He begins: 'I am sitting in the big red chair in my living-room . . . . ' etc. With his permission, and *after* he has had opportunity to learn the value of self-observation through the initial interview and scale, I will play back to him the recording of his statement on tape.

Thus in the first instance, Tom has the chance to relive once more a particular segment of his experiences of last night, with a view to observing these later.

The reliving of such experience is not, however, the same as having experienced it twenty-four hours ago. Firstly, because he is in fact sitting in *my* office twenty-four hours later; and secondly, because he is sharing his experience *with me.* He does not talk just to a tape-recorder but to another human being. These two factors supply a greater sense of security, because they convey to him that he has survived last night's experiences, and however much he may recall positive and negative reactions to those experiences, even if he uses the present tense, last night has gone and today is another day. While last night Tom was alone with his life, today he is not. I am with him. He can also allow himself to feel all that he *was* feeling, because he knows that I shall keep him within the framework of that half-hour and that if he wanders away too far I shall bring him back.

Tom also knows from past experience with me that I shall not allow him to be crushed by his experiences. My being there with him allows him to lower his defences so that he can move within the headlights of his own speed, knowing that someone else may use the brakes if it becomes necessary. But, precisely for this reason, *my* using *his* brakes becomes unnecessary. He knows that I trust him and I know that he trusts me. This mutual trust, in relation to the events of his past twenty-four hours, gives him an increased sense of security and self-confidence. The unspoken words are as follows: 'I know that you would not want me to be overwhelmed by what I am experiencing, or have experienced, and that you trust me to be able to cope with what I am saying. Because I trust you, and because you trust me, I feel much safer, and allow myself to go as far as I am able.'

When after a few minutes, I asked him to imagine himself at the age of sixty, and to reflect on how he had been able to overcome his problems with his wife in relation to that particular episode that he had presented for examination, there are two further important developments taking place.

1) Placing him into an imagined future does not, of course, mean that he had in fact produced premonitions about that future. It simply means that, by projecting himself in imagination further ahead, he can detach himself from the chaotic present. Tom does not enter the future, but he is enabled to use his experiences from the past more effectively.

2) The fact that he can give himself advice as to what he may have to do in the near future (i.e. to find some way of communicating with his wife) also does not come from future experiences that have not yet taken place. It comes from two sources: (a) that conceivably (by placing him into the future) *there is* a future, and (b) that he thinks constructively about solutions regarding something definite (i.e. his statement), instead of thinking about these things with confusion or destructively.

I say to him: 'What I am asking you to do is to allow your young self facing your old self to reflect on how the old man had solved his problem.'

Tom, of course, could have answered: 'The old man had not solved the problem at all.' But in fact my question aimed at solution, and experience shows that most people try to find solutions, even if at times this is very difficult for them.

This does not mean that such perceived solutions will in fact be carried out. There is a greater chance of solving problems, however, if ways of solution are conceived of than there is if such solutions are not put to the test.

As Tom reflects on how his old self in fact coped with the defined statement, he uses the past tense: 'I did it by finally doing something . . . . ' In a sense therefore the imagined solution is being presented *as if it has already happened.* Tom had experience not only of what happened to him between 6.30 and 7 on the previous evening, but he also had experience (although imagined) of how he had coped with this experience. The fact that he had the feeling that his projected solution had already happened gave him a greater sense of hope that he might actually carry it out some time after the interview. He said: 'Eventually we had reached agreement [he and his wife] with each other, so that when things are getting out of hand we would have a contract to sit down and start talking about our differences and our problems . . . . '

Without hope, there cannot be any steps towards solutions in the human situation.

Having experienced himself as having solved his problems, the next thing I asked him to do was to go back in memory to an actual event that took place when he was a child. I further asked him to allow that child to approach the thirty-six-year-old adult: 'I would like you to have a little conversation with the child and find out if he ever thought that he would get married one day and whether this is the way that *you* had imagined it, as it is . . . . '

Two factors should be considered here: (1) that Tom had chosen an actual event from his childhood; and (2) that this event also is being connected to last night's statement.

Tom could have chosen from thousands of experiences from his past. It is not a coincidence, however, that he chose one in which he did something wrong, or was thought by his father to have done something wrong. Punishment followed. He experienced a great feeling of loneliness. He says: 'Now at the age of thirty-six I have found that you can have an equally lonely life although you have a wife around.'

To connect past, present and future in relation to an actual recent event helps the integrating process to take place, and connections are made by the patient both during, and particularly after, the interview. The impact of this process, and often the short experience of treatment (this particular treatment session lasted for about an hour), is very considerable, particularly during the playback. The search for a final theme (always related to the presented statement) and the final attempt to define such a theme from all the recorded reactions (while listening to the tape) can have a far-reaching effect on future actions. The therapist must not rest until the patient is able to formulate some constructive plan from his summary-conclusions.

Often it is not necessary to use more than the actual statement events and to allow the patient to reflect and to make his tentative conclusions. There are, however, circumstances when a bridge between past, present and future must be built. From experience it has been found that the statement as a treatment method is not all that effective if the whole previous process of initial interview and scale has not been applied. It seems that these may be prerequisite to effective statement treatment.

## Summary notes on the statements

The exploration of a limited period allows the patient to choose what appears to him to be a significant event of his near past (last twenty-four hours). The statement of this experience allows the patient to share with the therapist the facts of those events and also his thoughts and feelings in connection with such facts.

Any human event contains elements of past events of the individual's life, and also past thoughts and feelings. As has been said earlier, man's present contains and defines his past experiences. Any *examinable* event, provided it can be viewed within a given framework of time, attracts associations from a more global past experience. The possibility of self-observation (through hearing oneself on the tape and/or reviewing the summaries written down) helps the process of self-integration, i.e. the connection of present with past, at least those aspects of such interaction that have relevance to that which is under examination. This process of integration can, and often does, fill the patient with a sense of meaning; i.e., however frag- mented the associations have been, in retrospect they now make sense. In consequence human experience can be re- viewed as a potential to present and future social func- tioning.

There are, of course, many patients with whom I would not attempt this method. These may be individuals who for a number of reasons are either incapable of self-observation or for whom such observations may convey only negative mean- ing. In the case of severe depression, for example, when the ego is flooded by the id, I would not attempt to do the statement. Depending on how much ego strength is avail- able and how far the patient is capable of selecting not only negative but also positive elements of conclusions, the state- ment may or may not be carried out. It is the patient's own pace and ability to integrate that will decide whether or not such a technique should be used. I must have a great deal of personal knowledge and observation of the patient either during the initial interview or through his scale reactions before I will attempt to undertake this treatment. I would never force the patient into any therapeutic situation that is for any reason not acceptable to him.

I find it very important, therefore, that when such addi- tional therapeutic measures are undertaken the therapist should have a thorough training in the psychotherapeutic methods other than those that I have described so far. After all, I do not regard the methods that I am describing as alternatives to other psychotherapeutic practices, but rather as additional techniques. Again, I would like to emphasize that after training in the methods that I have des- cribed here, and will be describing in the next chapter, each individual therapist will have to use his or her knowledge and to *fit in* these practices when applicable according to his or her judgement of the case.

# 6 The Dialogue

From the earliest days of prehistory, men have attempted to formulate a meaning to their lives and have sought ways of defining this meaning. So-called primitive man looked beyond himself, trying to seek answers to questions that were sometimes formulated and sometimes not. Spirits and gods were given the power of superhuman and often extra-terrestrial nature. Such powers 'spoke' to man, directed his actions, laid down laws and measured out punishment in case of breaking them.

There were always the chosen few, even in those early days, who had had direct communication with such spirits, demons and gods. They interpreted the meaning of events to man as they perceived the messages from beyond most men's comprehension. As primitive man perceived the world in this 'reality' he also perceived and accepted the reality of the interpretations beyond his comprehension by these magical men, and they themselves accepted that they were in direct communication with the demons, the spirits and the gods. As far as their subjective experience goes, they believed the reality of their claim, and reality of all kinds is always subjective.

The point for us is not to consider whether primitive men were deluded or not, but whether they were genuine about their beliefs. Anthropologists would confirm that in some way perhaps they were even more genuine about them than we are today about our beliefs. It can be argued, of course, that these early men had been in touch with nothing but their own unconscious. This argument may stand to reason. The ultimate question, however, that we have to pose is whether or not it helped man for him to be in touch with whatever forces spoke from within him?

Whatever interpretation we may give to early religious beliefs, we must accept that primitive man was genuinely in touch with some kind of a source, unconscious or not, and that this source was capable of guidance, and that it created a world for man beyond his immediate environment.

Whether we have developed spiritually or emotionally since those early days remains a great question. Technical

achievement does not mean that man has evolved either emotionally or spiritually. The events of the last five thousand
years show clearly that the savage exists in modern man, and
because of technical superiority he is capable of being even
more savage than his so-called savage ancestors.

What is man in touch with today that extends beyond his
own environment? Owing to his vast technical and intellectual
development, man has increasingly lost touch with those
forces that operated in his ancestors. The dialogue between
himself and his gods seems to have evaporated across the
passing centuries. Today if any normal man or woman were to
state publicly that he or she is in touch with such forces this
would be considered a sign of mental illness. Our age of reason
has stopped the dialogue between man and his gods.

From a purely logical point of view, or if one likes to call
it a scientific point of view, this dialogue between man and
the beyond can be considered a dialogue between man's
experience (conscious and unconscious), his hopes, aspirations
and search for personal meaning. If we are not to enter into
the question of ultimate reality (whether or not God exists),
but examine only the need for the dialogue, then modern
man is in a bad shape. The need for man to communicate and
understand himself as part of the world and perhaps the
cosmos is as old as man himself, and denial of the need is
not the end of the need.

Irrespective of whether man reaches out towards God or
not, *he must reach himself.* The external world will not
satisfy man's basic need for meaning. He therefore must be
given a chance and opportunity to collect his experiences,
aspirations and hopes into some kind of unity. Man needs to
create a powerful magnet from the particles of his experiences with which he can be in touch, which can advise him in
times of turmoil, fill his life with meaning and purpose, and
move towards the centuries to come. Otherwise it will be (and
already is) easy for him to lose himself among the things
that he has created, and *things* have no meaning except use.
A washing machine is useful but does not answer urgent
questions on, say, the problems of middle-age. Man cannot
have a dialogue with a television set. The process of 'magnet-
ization', the bringing together of experience consisting of

early fairy tales, anxieties, fears, hopes, bewilderment, wonder, beauty and ugliness into a meaningful whole, is what the dialogue in a therapeutic sense attempts to achieve.

How can we bring together into a powerful unit most of what we are? And provided we have been successful in bringing these together, how can we begin to use this vast magnet to help us through life and give us some aim and purpose for the future? In order to do this one would need to personify past experience in such a way that eventually one has direct access to the totality of such personification.

The dialogue cannot properly be called a treatment method. Although with selected cases it may help the therapeutic process, the dialogue is a growth process and it is applicable to those who have lost their aim and purpose in life, or who feel an emptiness that needs to be fulfilled. In a sense it is an educational process with a difference. Education aims at increasing experience through learning, hoping that ultimately such experience can be applied to some aspect of living. The dialogue, on the contrary, makes use of already learned experiences, attempting to unify these into a kind of synthesis. In fact, it is a confrontation with one's more global experiences. Access to these experiences is possible only if I can create a framework or a container from which such synthetized experience can be drawn. One way in which I may be able to achieve such a synthesis is through a *paraphasis,* i.e. through talking to or being in touch with the synthesis of my experiences. Therefore that framework which I can 'talk to', or which can 'talk to me', is called a paraphant. The paraphant thus becomes the container of my experiences, and provided I learn some patterns of communication with it (or with him or her) it can crystallize and it can potentially answer some of the problems that I am faced with.

There are, however, a number of conditions that are essential in order to achieve a paraphasis.

1) I must trust that my life so far, with all its positive and negative experiences, does add up to potential meaning; in short, that my life so far has the potential of a guide to the future or the potentiality to become a guide for my future.

2) I have achieved so far in my life certain transforma-

tions of frustrations into satisfactions, and this, up to a point, has been my 'spur'.

3) I attempt this search for my personal paraphant through a trained and skilled guide (in a sense we can call him a therapist, or a mixture of therapist and teacher), who has achieved the personification of his own experiences and who has the skill and training to help his patient to differentiate attempts at true solutions from wishful thinking.

In the dialogue, what ultimately matters is that I am capable of drawing on the millions of experiences that, hitherto split and sometimes isolated, exist in my past (and/or in my unconscious) and because of this splitting I hitherto had no access, or only partial access, to their wisdom.

It is not a coincidence that in psychosis, and particularly in schizophrenia, such split aspects of experiences break through from the unconscious and force an independent 'voice' on the sufferer. The difference between paraphasis and hallucination is this: in hallucination the voices or voice appears involuntarily. In paraphasis it is introduced voluntarily and one is not in contact with split parts but with totality.

Paraphasis is not only an artificial method that has arisen from the work carried out in human social functioning, but it is the most natural and creative aspect alive in man. The small child who talks to her doll or the little boy who creates the world of imagination in which he can act out and externalize internal processes are in fact practising this creative process.

But what happens to this magic of the creativity of our early years as the grey years of adulthood slowly descend upon us? We may begin to deny the most precious within our human experience by dismissing it as being childish, and in this process, as Dr R. D. Laing* describes it, we lose touch with the magical quality of our early years. If the pressures in the external world are too great to make us deny the existence of an inner creative world, and if, owing to these pressures, we are incapable of using anything constructive or

* R.D. Laing, *The Politics of Experience and the Bird of Paradise* (Harmondsworth 1967).

creative, the potential of our creativity, followed by increased frustration, will reach a point when such creativity breaks into consciousness, as is the case in schizophrenia.

It may then be that schizophrenia is a protest against frustration, a loss of hope of achieving creativity; then it is possible that the inoculation against such internal denigration can be achieved throughout life through educators and others keeping alive the paraphasis. Then men and women to whom humdrum work will not be satisfying would still have the alternative for self-expression even if this would not be the source of livelihood. Then it would not be necessary in later years to bring about so-called experts to help man to get in touch again with that lost world of beauty.

It is somewhat difficult to describe the actual process of the dialogue, because this is always unique to the individual; yet there are some common features that are valid. The dialogue attempts, as I have said, to put man in touch with his more global experiences, to which he has no access at the point of time when he seeks help. This help is invariably in connection with meaning and purpose, lost hope, bewilderment and what life is all about. The dialogue is the bridge and should not be considered as the final answer. It allows man to draw on his experiences, after which he may use such knowledge in his daily existence in any way *he* thinks fit.

### Dialogue with Eva (case no 5)
(Age 57, widow)

Since her husband's death five years before our meeting, this still lovely-looking white-haired woman became more and more withdrawn and had lost interest in living. At first her depression was understood to be a reaction to her husband's death, but as time went on, instead of the feeling of isolation and hopelessness decreasing, it had increased. It was not a clinical depression in a true sense: Eva did not slow down; she did not lose her appetite. She just became increasingly aware that, apart from the support of her husband, something was missing from her life, and she described it thus: 'This something has been missing even while I was married but I was too busy to take notice of it.'

On occasions before our meeting, as she reflected on the events of her past, she felt she could not complain. It had been a good life as far as it went, apart from ups and down in her marriage, and one particular crisis while she was still very young when her husband left home for a few months and lived with someone else. She did not think that her life was useless. On occasions she had thought during those past years that perhaps there should be more to it than bringing up her two children and looking after the wellbeing of her husband (he apparently greatly regretted his leaving her, and she in time had forgiven if not forgotten that painful event). She did not feel that it was a medical problem that she should be helped with. She felt that doctors could not answer any of the problems she had faced.

What were these problems? It really always boiled down to the same thing. Had she done with her life what she was capable of doing? And more so, could she do something more meaningful with her life now and in the future? Her children had their own lives, and although the relationship with them was fairly good she did not feel that she should be imposing on them. Somehow marriage as a solution to her problem did not seem feasible. If somebody turned up who was nice and loving she would have no objection, but there was something in her and in her own right that demanded admission and she did not know what this something was.

In the initial interview, and subsequently when observing her scale structure, she did not clarify anything that she did not know before. It appeared to her that no amount of reflection on the present or past would give the answer, yet there was an answer somewhere.

One day, as we were discussing some of this, and she was telling me that our exercise together was leading her nowhere, she began to talk about some episode or episodes in her early childhood. She recalled the night, and how the moonlight shone through the window on to her mother's dressing-gown which was hanging on the door. She was probably half asleep when this dressing-gown began to become alive, grew into a kind of large doll, a mixture of fairy and witch, sometimes this and sometimes that, and carried her beyond her room into the world outside. She visited a number of people and places, some known to her and some unknown. As she recalled this she turned to me suddenly and said: 'Now you see, if only I could believe in the magic of that dressing-gown again . . . . ' and she went on to say that truly as she reflects on the events of those strange evenings in her past, the combination of the moon shining on the dressing-gown and the light from the street had given a quality of life to it. 'Would you consider me crazy if I did a little exercise?' she asked. 'What exercise?' was my response. She went on: 'I see in front of me not that dressing-gown *but that which I made of it*. That fairy and that witch. Even to this day and at this moment it really represents to me not only the magic of my experiences then but somehow a knowledge . . . . '

I did not understand.

She went on: 'If I addressed that fairy now and asked her for advice I bet anything that I could get some answers.'

This controlled woman now suddenly got very excited about this possibility but she was very shy and cautious lest I might think that she had gone completely off her rocker. I said to her: 'Why not? If those early images in your life can give you an answer to your present predicament, why not?'

So a dialogue began between herself and now the fairy and now the witch. After so many years I cannot recall the details, but I remember only the impact made upon me by this that appeared to be a monologue but in fact for her was a dialogue. It was like a fairy tale enacted. Now she would say something like this: 'Where have I lost my turning?' And the fairy apparently answered: 'Precisely because you got away from me; because you did not believe any more that miracles are around the corner.'

I listened for some time with great fascination to this exercise. I must admit that for some time I was in doubt; it is so easy to be in doubt. When man confronts the unconscious in himself, and with my particular training in psychiatry, I was seriously wondering if this was not in fact a form of hallucination. The process, however, was very different from anything that I had observed with psychotic patients. Those patients never ask questions and receive answers whether they wish to or not. Here the questions and answers seemed to come from some source or sources where questions were clearly formulated and answers were clearly given. The whole process did not go on longer than about ten minutes and I saw this woman smile for the first time after it was over. She said: 'I know now what I have to do, you know.' I remember that there was a considerably long silence and I remember too that my curiosity was increasing, when she turned to me: 'What stops me from writing these things down; the early memories as well as the ones that I would imagine now? What would stop me from writing fairy tales?'

'Nothing [I answered] except that I do not understand why this has not occurred to you before.'

'It did [she said] but I have never been in touch since those days with the fairy and the witch. Now I have been.'

This happened in the late 1950s. Since then she has written a number of stories, and the change as a result in her personal life and in her attitude to life is beyond recognition. The combination of the fairy and the witch became the paraphant, that which supplied the source of her experiences, that which had become the container of her experiences through which she could use the pains and revelations and beauties of her own life.

We can attempt to compare the dialogue with computer programming. The computer has access, through the in-fed information, to the results of such information by drawing the thousands or millions of components together into an answer. But however much information has been fed into a human being, only a fraction of this is accessible to him at any given time. Here the comparison with the computer comes to an end. Computers can react only to actual information fed into them; they are not capable of registering such feelings and reactions as human beings experience even if only momentarily as they pass through time. If then one calls upon oneself to utilize experience it is not only that one needs to have access to facts. It is still impossible, even with a gift for paraphasis, to have access to totality; all one can achieve is access to more global experiences of the past. Furthermore, not everyone is capable of evolving a paraphant. People whose imagination has been unused or blocked throughout the process of growing up may not be able to make any sense of the process of the dialogue. In short, the dialogue can be used only by people who have a potential capacity for *creative imagination.*

From experience it seems that educational achievements are less relevant here than the capacity for creative imagination. It is also possible (although there is less evidence for this so far) that fantasy might turn into creative imagination, provided the ego can register differences between reality and fantasy. To those for whom fantasy is their reality, paraphasis becomes an impossibility, and very great care should be taken in the process of interviewing, and in using the scale in treatment, to establish whether or not any given patient is capable of differentiating. The basic principle is that it is the patient, rather than the therapist, who defines the method, and if the patient is consciously or unconsciously reluctant to go along with this process of self-observation, then the therapist must at all times respect this.

The actual time for the dialogue, i.e. the imaginative excursion, should never exceed fifteen to twenty minutes, and should always be followed by replay, so that the patient may be able to differentiate between wishful thinking on the one hand and attempts at real solutions on the other. As in any other method of treatment, at the end one must attempt to arrive at a theme or message that is significant for the patient's day-to-day living. Unless recognition through access to earlier experiences is related to the ordinary course of living (i.e. changed attitude towards objects and persons), no real measurement of change has taken place. Change can be evaluated only through changed life patterns. If as a result of the dialogue a positive *feeling* is forthcoming but no actual change takes place in the style or pattern of life, then one must view any result with suspicion.

The following two cases will be illustrations of an unsuccessful and a successful dialogue process.

## Dialogue with Norman (case no 6)
(Age 55, married, three children, lecturer)

Norman's main problem was that he did not show up well at promotion interviews. While he himself perceived his abilities as above the rank given to him in the academic framework where he had been functioning, the senior members of his team apparently did not have an identical or similar perception of him. Apart from such clash of perception of his abilities or otherwise, he was constantly criticized by his colleagues for 'keeping things to himself' - i.e., he was not communicative, did not share his views with others; at meetings he tended to be rather quiet and then when issues were not important at all he 'made a fuss' over things that seemed to matter less to his colleagues than they apparently did to him. They accused him of being unable to differentiate between what was, and what was not, important, and said that he was either obsessional about certain minor issues or else incapable of grasping matters of significance at all.

On the personal front, Norman's marriage was described by him as a catastrophe. He complained that his wife 'even at her age [similar age to that of the patient] was not really interested in anything else except sex'. Although they had lived together for a great many years and except for the youngest (a girl) the children were away from home, he still felt that his wife did not care about the children and accused her (without much evidence) of periodically being unfaithful to him. He said that the only satisfaction he had was when he was together with his students, who appreciated him and who themselves felt deeply concerned about his failure to receive promotion and recognition. He very much identified himself with the dissatisfaction that students had expressed, and although not supporting their cause in public had certainly supported them within the student-teacher relationship.

Having gone through a number of interviews, including the use of the scale, he still could not see himself as others perceived him, and at one point he expressed some interest 'at least to have a clue as to what they really see in me'. He then proceeded to speak about the nature of wisdom in rather philosophical terms and said that human history shows that really wise men had seldom been recognized in their own time. In fact he claimed that he had been a sacrifice 'on the altar of science'.

As he wished to see himself as others perceived him, we built up together the framework where such self-examination could become a possibility. It was to be an interview situation when he had to attend a panel that was to decide whether or not he should receive promotion. There are four people in the room. They are sitting in a semi-circle. One is a man with glasses (he mentioned his name). The head of the department has a writing-pad in front of him. (It should be remembered that although he had attended a number of such or similar interviews, in the dialogue he is placed into an imagined situation, i.e. one which he is making up during the process of the dialogue. For example, the head of the department had never interviewed him in the past - this he made up during the process.)

He said: 'In that semi-circle I am placed opposite the window, and a light - sunshine - somehow blurs my vision. I would like to ask them to allow me to sit in another chair, but I think that they might think badly of me if I made that request, so I just sit there feeling uneasy and nervous. One interviewer, a man who is much younger than myself [this particular person is a colleague, someone who had in fact taken part in some previous interview process] asks me why I think I should be promoted. He puts it this way: "Why do you think you should be given promotion?" The word *think* makes me rather angry. What the hell does he mean by saying *think*? This immediately conveys to me that he does not think that I should be promoted. So what can I do? Trying to cover up my anger, I answer simply: "I am here because I should be promoted." They look at each other and the head makes some note on the writing-pad. My answer obviously was wrong, yet to me it is right. "All right [says the former interviewer], why should you be promoted?" I say: "I have done some original work. I have been able to communicate whatever I know to my students. I have spent a great deal of time at this establishment and others who to my mind have done less have already been promoted." Again the man with the glasses writes something down.'

As he listens back to the tape he has no reactions whatsoever until the very end. They he says: 'I do actually see that my anger does communicate itself and that if I place myself into their shoes they would pick up my anger and frustration rather than my ability. I do not seem to be making my point. I do not seem to communicate myself to them. But how can I *when I have these feelings?* When I resent the very fact of being interviewed?'

I said: 'Well how can you?'

He said: 'I resent this system of interviewing. I resent the fact that people whose knowledge and understanding is less than mine can make decisions about my future. Short of being a double-faced bastard I cannot think of how I could survive such interviews. Do I have to become a bastard?'

'You spoke of wisdom before [I said]. Could you not think of a wise man, whom you would make up now out of what you consider from past experience to be wisdom, and address this question to him?'

After a few minutes' silence he said, half-smiling: 'I see a character; it is somewhere in Greece, he is a kind of combination of Socrates and Plato, he is dressed in white, has white long hair, looks like a hippie, an aged hippie. You want me to ask him about what?'

I said: 'If *you* want to formulate your question which, if I remember rightly, was: 'Do I have to become a bastard?' or if you formulate it in any other way, you might be able to draw on your experiences via this Greek sage that you have made up.'

'So you want to know [he said] what my question would be!'

I said: 'Unless one formulates a question clearly one cannot receive an answer, either from others or from oneself.'

After some minutes of silence, he said: 'All right, then the question will be: "Do I have to hide my real feelings before the members of the interviewing committee?" '

I asked: 'What do you mean by feelings?'

'All right! Do I have to hide my aggression? No! *Can* I hide my aggression?'

He now addresses himself to this paraphant but to his great surprise the Greek sage turns away and is not answering him. 'He just sits there and turns his back to me. What do you make of it?'

I put the question back to him: 'What do *you* make of it?'

'I would say that this is a silly game or else that I cannot call an answer, I cannot *provoke* an answer. I have no access to such an answer.'

As he once more listens to the tape the word he used, provoke, becomes significant to him. 'How can you have a bloody answer if you provoke?'

He left it at that and although at that time he felt that he understood the nature of his provoking manner (both with the sage and at interviews) he still was not able to modify his feelings in subsequent interview situations.

Norman presented as his main problem his inability to get promotion. While he had registered some other problems in his life, including a 'catastrophic marriage', at the time leading up to the dialogue Norman's preoccupation was with his frustrating work situation, and he skimmed over the other problems of his life.

Consistently through the initial interview, in his reaction to the scale, and to the dialogue too, he concentrated almost obsessionally on that one area. He had said at the previous interview that one of his reasons for concentrating on the work situation was that he could probably do something about that, whereas he could not do much about his marriage.

In the system I am describing one does not press the patient to review an area which, although the *therapist* may recognize it as highly relevant, is not so recognized by the patient. In some other form of treatment methodology one would attempt to make some links; i.e., the therapist would guide the patient to make connections between the possibility of a failure in marriage and his anger because of the impotency of his situation and that of taking it out on, say, colleagues and the interviewing committee. Furthermore, in some other form of psychodynamic or psychoanalytical treatment such anger or aggression would manifest itself not only in relation to persons in the patient's life-situation, but also in relation to the therapist. The therapist then could, through skilful interpretation of this transference, help the patient to make connections not only between, say, two interacting areas of his life (i.e. marriage and work), but also within the transference between his feelings for or against the therapist and that of earlier life experiences which are the springboard of such present patterns. Such treatment invariably would take a very long time; and while results cannot be predicted, it can be assumed that in many cases such 'chimney-sweeping' (to use Freud's own early terminology) may be very effective. The issue in such cases as that of Norman is whether or not one ought to consider and/or suggest referral to this kind of psychotherapeutic treatment method, because there is no denying that while the methods described here are effective (and sometimes very effective) with large numbers of people, they are not invariably effective with all people. In fact, if social functioning methods are effective they are usually so in short-term treatment whose results to start with are also unpredictable.

Experience shows that on the other hand there are a number of patients who have had psychoanalytical treatment for a great many years, and yet still retain a residue of problems which, *after* such treatment, social functioning methodology may clear up or at least deal with to a greater satisfaction to the patient.

The method suggested here does not claim to be a unique method, a cure for all, but rather one where the patient (provided he can make use of his own advice and his own experiences) may find alternative solutions for his predicament. There should be therefore a close link between all existing treatment methods. Patients should not find themselves unable to benefit later on from the use of some other method if my suggestions are not altogether successful.

In the case of Norman, I did suggest to him at our last meeting that he might find it useful to seek a treatment which, although it might take much longer, could bring him face to face with the cause of his present life pattern.

There are some further considerations from the case of Norman. What are the contributing factors to the ability to make connections and/or the inability to make such connections? In Norman's case he chose an area (work) which he thought, rightly or wrongly, as more managable for him than, say, his marriage. In consequence he has become fixated on the area of work and promotion.

When in the past I had been dealing with a large group of unemployed men who had lost their employment for reasons beyond their control (i.e. factories closed down or moved away, and they could not for personal reasons move to the place or places where employment was available), a reactive depression overwhelmed the ability to keep working and earn one's living, and the result was an overall reaction to other life areas including that of marriage. Many men, particularly those about the age of forty, who had lost their jobs, as a result of such reactive depression had become sexually impotent, often in a hitherto stable marriage situation. The sexual complication added to a general inability to take on employment even when this was offered in the *same* locality, several months later. Unless the marital area was cleared up, such patients could not take advantage of any given work situation. They become extremely aggressive with the officials of the state, on whom they attempted to displace their bitterness. Such people, too, like Norman, had presented their work situation as the visible part of the iceberg and could seldom see or acknowledge connections between marital and work areas.

In most of such situations, however, there was one basic difference to that of Norman's situation: that the marriage had been stable and that the wives themselves had been trying to help their husbands with their more personal problems. The wives very often sought me out, often with little bitterness, and one could give *them* help to enable them to help their partners to solve, even if slightly, some of the problems in relation to marriage and sex. In many cases, then, once the wives had received help, the husbands were able to make the necessary steps back towards employment, thus re-establishing the pattern that had been disturbed by redundancy.

In Norman's case (although his problem was not identical

with these redundancy men), he could not have the help of his wife in connection with his problems because as far as the wife was concerned the marriage had been over for many years. It is in some ways even doubtful whether it had ever started.

In Case 1 (page 35), Mr X was able to use the interviewing techniques to make a decision to bring what he considered to be his unsatisfactory marriage to an end. Norman was unable to do this. Why can one man use more global life experiences to make decisions than another? Whatever answers one would give would be speculative, and therefore I will not attempt to formulate such answers. I simply must register that Norman was quite unable to do so.

*Dialogue with F.R. (case 7)*
(Age 39, businessman, married, two children)
[F.R. said:] It appears to me that a period of my life has ended. I have struggled throughout for financial independence and I have achieved it, in some ways more so than I had anticipated. You see, when I left school there were two possibilities open to me. The first was to go to university, but honestly I did not think that I'd got it; I certainly did not feel that I would be happy there, or frankly that my intellectual abilities were such that I could succeed, despite my mother's having such aspirations for me. My father was more realistic. He said: 'Go into business and you will make it there.' So this was the second choice. Oddly enough I was not too keen on business either, but once I started in a business, where many others had failed because it had been highly competitive, I decided that I would make a success of it. I told you that I did this. Without apology I would say that if I did not do a stroke of work from this moment on I could live quite comfortably for the rest of my life. Was I lucky or single-minded? Both! But beyond that, there was something else too. I learned the skills and know-how, if you see what I mean. But it was a bloody rat-race. It still is. The only difference between then and now is that it hurts me now.

I shall be forty next year, and the years force me to recognize and accept the fact of the on-coming middle-age. Wishful thinking, regret, fear, anxiety will not change this fact and its subsequent implications. I was greatly shaken about a year ago when my wife became very ill. I love her more than I can say and I get embarrassed, and you see I have tears in my eyes when I speak about her. I thought: 'She is going to die', but, thank God, she survived. During those weeks and months I walked the streets as if in a nightmare. Inside me I have rebelled against her illness, as it is one's human right to be healthy. There is no right in life, I find now, except living while it lasts. When she came back from the hospital we had some problems with our daughters, but again this also turned out to be all right. We have twins and they reacted very differently to their mother's long absence. Peggy completely withdrew into herself and Irene became very destructive, but it passed. It is good to be well off. God only knows what I would have done if I had not been. I got a middle-aged woman, a refugee, into the house to look after them, and I looked after her. By the way, I still do, although we have no actual need for her now.

During my wife's illness I became aware of the (please do not think that I exaggerate) ultimate isolation and loneliness. Some things opened in me that I wish to God would never have opened. You can call it depression if you like but I was depressed quite often in my life because of some difficulties in business or in the family, but never have I experienced this utter isolation.

There was once a dream a long time ago back at home in Lancashire, a dream that I belonged and that people cared. Have you ever been up there? People are kinder than here in the south; perhaps during the great upheaval of the 1930s poverty had thrown them towards each other. Now here in London people had shown themselves differently to me. I once read an article about the effect that some drug, I forget which, may have on people. This bloke walked on a New York street and saw expressions on people's faces that almost drove him into suicide. I was now that bloke, without having taken drugs. I see things so differently from the dream in which people were kind and warm and caring.

While she was in hospital I realized that practically everyone was using me under the guise of my Christian upbringing. I seldom said 'no' to people who needed me, and I have done a few things which perhaps I could be proud of. With my money, I mean. But when I was alone in London and I needed companionship I found invariably that people only wanted me for what I had, not for what I was. There were smiling faces around me, but would they still have smiled if I had been poor and penniless?

During those lonely weeks, long and lonely nights, questions came into my head which I could not even put into words, though everything on the face of it is now as it was before. If I want to have things I can buy them. If I decided that I wanted to go around the world I could do it tomorrow. All the things that this crazy society has created - perhaps not all, but most - I could buy. But what is the point? In fact what is the point of anything?

What I had missed with my interrupted education I tried to put right. The Greeks interested me greatly. They knew some questions and some answers. They knew too well that there is no ultimate peace on this side of Hades.

I still love her - my wife - and the twins, and yet I don't know what to do with myself. I can't carry on with my business, and as a result of what I feel, however warm the relationship is within the family, I feel like a stranger. You may find this silly - stupid, or crazy - but sometimes when this peculiar mood gets hold of me I will drive out in the car to the place where I was born. The M1 is not exactly a relaxing drive. There are still a few people there from the old days. My mother died and my father lives quite comfortably not very far from us in London, and yet there is something I am looking for, particularly at night, when I walk the streets of the place where I was born, and then I can imagine that everything is as it should be. When I drive back and come home in the early hours of the morning I feel worse than when I started. My wife, I am sure, is convinced that I have a mistress. She accepts my explanation yet is unconvinced.

I was what people call a lucky man. Yes, lucky. But so what? I understand so little. I see some vague rules operating behind life and living, but what I call rules might be self-deception. Perhaps there is something behind or beyond this existence, and perhaps there is not; and I tell you I don't know more today than I did when I was a youngster. And yet these rules are all important to me. Integrity is such a rule. As I say the word it sounds all funny, but I can tell you that although I was a business man I can still look into my own eyes without shame. No, perhaps that is not quite true, but let me say without much shame.

Can you understand what I am trying to tell you? I am not sick or mentally ill - at least I don't think I am. But I am concerned about the emptiness of my life, and it is no bloody good telling myself that I should not be empty: I am! Emptiness is evil and evil people destroy themselves, and if given half a chance they will destroy others too. Is there some order in life, even if I cannot decipher what it is? Is there more to it than meets the eye? This is what I came to see you about,

about this emptiness. Oh! I could go on living, and I certainly would not end my life, but what is living without life? If that makes any sense! Well, let me put it this way: is this tour across life a conducted tour? My life-experiences advise me that it is not, and yet it may be. I am looking for a God but I would hate to delude myself; that really would be terrible.

Let us have no false humility about it. I have achieved more than most people. In their eyes I am a great success. You know what I would like - to be given the opportunity to peep through the keyhole of life and just see what is on the other side. Nothing? or confusion? or what? And if there is something, then it would be worth it, and then it occurs to me that *he* said something about there being 'many rooms in my father's mansion', so even if I could peep into one, what would I see when there are so many? Or is it all nonsense?

When I was a young child I believed in God. I was taught to believe. Teaching without example teaches very little, but I had such an example: my parents were such an example. So you see I am lucky. Sometimes on TV there are these programmes about why people become criminals, and crazy, because they have had unhappy childhoods. I didn't! So now I have been talking all the time and I don't quite know what I am saying but it has got something to do with having lost the road. I would like to go somewhere but I don't know where.

I listened to all this without interruption. And as he was so deeply involved with what he was saying, and as it appeared to me that there were no natural breaks, I did not interrupt him or attempt to sum up either. What he said was in fact a summary itself. Now at the end, however, I said to him:

Let me try very briefly to take out the essential features of what you have told me. You are a successful businessman and have made a financial success of your life. Your wife's illness, more than ever, opened up dimensions in you which hitherto were lying dormant. You found in consequence that life and people were not as they had appeared to you when you were a child. You felt that you were used because you have money and when you needed people you felt they gave their attention to you only because you were rich. You tried to recover something of your past by driving up north, and although your wife is healthy now you feel emptiness not in relation to your family but in connection with your future, which may still hold the key. Would you say that this is a fair summary, or have I not understood you?

(He thought about this for some time and then he said:)

It is a fair summary but what you, of course, cannot express, and I would not expect you to be able to do so, is this strange feeling of coldness, being cut off, isolation, this beastly face of people. But apart from that, what you have said rings true.

(And again after a while he said:)

Towards the end you mentioned the word 'future'. I did not mention that word but you really are right. The big question is, what am I going to do tomorrow and the day after that? And how am I going to find out when all this time I could not do it myself?

Ten days later we did his scale profiles and he looked for the connections in his life areas. Despite what he had said he scored quite high on the positive index. The relationship between the positive and negative indexes (see chapter 2, pp. 22 - 3 ) was still within the bounds of norm although he had carried more than one-third frustration in relation to his satisfaction, but his synthesis score was considerably lower than that of the positive index. It was, therefore, as he himself said, not so much a crisis of the present, but truly a crisis regarding the future. He made two important connections, i.e. important to himself.
1) What were his feelings really in relation to his wife? He knew that they loved each other, but was not something missing?
2) The second connection he had made which he felt was important was his relationship with people; as he reflected on the friendship and persecution scores he felt that there was not even one person he could really and truly call a friend. Why was that? Was it he himself who prevented it? Was it that he was so much involved with the family that he had no place for others? What the hell was it all about?

As he looked at the summary of summaries he said: 'What I need to explore is what I can offer people apart from money!'

*Further dialogue with F.R.*

A spark of gift has been my constant companion across the years. My early fantasies (or were they imaginations?) may or may not have been due to some Oedipus or other complex, but as I look back they definitely foretold things to come. 'The King and I' - that is a game I used to play, being a king. This game has been with me as a constant companion, except that I now play the game with different toys.

There appears to be a continuity running through my life. Throughout the years I had learned not to let people down. I haven't ever regretted it. I have paid as much attention to so-called small men as I have done to big ones. Although I am a businessman one of my failings has been that I had trusted people too much, yet even this trust caused only momentary disappointments. But I have often been disappointed that, when I told my friends my aspirations and ambitions, they could not understand my dreams - but how could they, when they did not even know their own dreams?

Integrity is very important to me but it is also important to know how to play the game. Without this knowledge most men of integrity still would be crucified.

This interview took place before Christmas and he was thinking how far the symbol of that significant birth of almost two thousand years ago had influenced him during this particular interview. He also said that a title could be given to his contemplations: 'Some Thoughts on Life'.

I tried to sum up at this point what he had said so far:

If I have understood you correctly you had been gifted since you can recall and that this represents a continuity in your life. You said that you have attempted to pay attention to all kinds of people, and although you have been disappointed in some, these were only temporary disappointments. If I remember correctly, you also said that you have been disappointed because your friends could not share your dreams. Integrity is of importance to you but you have also learned how to 'play the game'. And finally, you are wondering how far this is all dissipated by the on-coming Christmas and your feelings about the birth of Jesus.

(After a long pause he continued, without reacting verbally to my summary   he just nodded.)

*F.R.* There are rules and laws operating within and without. I must learn to know these and to respect them. One can, I suppose, stretch this law, but one cannot, must not, break it. The breaking of the law would destroy me. You mentioned Jesus. The thought occurs to me that death can exist among the living. I know a number of dead men who are walking about. They are dead inside, because they have never respected anything, including themselves. Yet real death may very well be a part of living. The threat to me is not real death but being dead while I am alive.

You told me last time when I had looked at the scale profiles that you were ultimately left with my question as to what I need to explore; or to put it differently, what I can offer to people apart from money. I still have not an answer to this. How am I going to be able to find one now that I have clarified the question?

*E.H.* Let me try once more to summarize what you have just said. Please correct me if my summary is not what you have told me.

You feel that there are some rules, or as you put it laws, operating in life, and that those who are alive know and respect these laws, and that you have known a number of people who were dead although to all appearances living. And you are asking the question, how can you find an answer to your formulation as to what you can offer people apart from your money.

*F.R.* One is a prostitute in a sense. One is prostituting a little talent; one might have to earn a living at something which one really despises. Perhaps despise is too strong a word. I would like to substitute the word 'empty'. I am as convinced as I can be by now that men want, above anything else, freedom, and that absolute belonging means the end of freedom. To be free means that one must not belong anywhere really, yet perhaps everywhere. But for God's sake I must belong to myself, and yet so far practically everything and everyone tells me what is good and what is bad for me. One of my great suspicions is of psychotherapy too - to fall into this trap, although I don't know very much about it. But if what you are doing is psychotherapy then here I seem to be kind of answering myself and that is precisely what is missing out there. They tell you that it is good for you to sell things, and the little voice inside says: 'It is not that good'.

(I interrupt:)

*E.H.* What little voice are you talking about?

*F.R.* You know, that which speaks when we are alone, if we only listen; but we are not allowed to listen.

*E.H.* You are allowed to listen now.

*F.R.* How to try to make this little voice a big voice? How?

*E.H.* Let us presume that I ask you to imagine that you are in a jungle; I mean literally in a jungle, and eventually you find an opening that leads you to a clearance, and then to a beach, and there you have the ocean beyond that beach. Could you imagine that on that beach there is a little hut and someone lives in that hut who moved himself away from the jungle, someone who would know all the answers to your questions? Can you see this picture?

*F.R.* My God, and how clearly! I am working my way through the jungle. I can really hear the animals and things making the kind of noise that I suppose exists in the jungle. There is an element of fear in me because the jungle is dangerous too, and incredibly beautiful. I do find that opening that you talked about. I do see the ocean. My God, the water is so very blue, and I do see that hut.

(Then he turned to me and asked:)

Do you want me to make up someone that lives in the hut? I suppose it will have to be somebody terribly old and wise. Who else would choose to live alone and away and content with his own company?

*E.H.* Go to the hut, seek out whoever is in there, and then try to put your question or questions to whom you find there.

*F.R.* The funny thing is that the whole thing is so clear. He is sitting in front of a kind of porch. He is terribly old [and he laughed]. If someone can be over a hundred years old then that bloke certainly is. His face is wrinkled and hundreds of lines are on it. He is quite tall and thin yet there is something about the movement of this old man which makes me feel that he is in some ways younger than I am, and I am certainly not several hundred years old. [He laughs] I don't know why but usually eastern sages don't have blue eyes; this old chappie certainly has. His eyes are as blue as the ocean. He is very friendly and he knows why I am there.

*E.H.* Ask him the question.

*F.R.* I am so taken by all this, Professor, that I am forgetting really what the question was! Now, what the hell was it? [He thinks very hard.] Oh yes, what can I offer people apart from my money? [He turns to me half-smiling.] You want me to ask him that?

*E.H.* Yes.

*F.R.* You seem to be very wise [now speaking to the sage]. What can I really offer to people? God, do you know what he is asking me?

*E.H.* What?

*F.R.* He is asking me to tell him what I have to offer. That is a difficult one. So I tell him, if I knew what I had to offer I would not ask him. He really is a kind old man. He smiles at me and he says: 'What you have to offer is what you are, and what you are you have been spelling out all your life, but particularly during the last few weeks. I could name you a few things that you are. You are gifted. You are a leader. Despite your success you are naive and vulnerable too. You have integrity but you are willing to compromise. You seek freedom only you find living, and yet you may very well be afraid that you are one of those dead men that you occasionally have the opportunity to observe; or at least if you are not yet, you are afraid that you will become one of those.

(He turned to me and said:)

This is quite incredible. This is not really a little voice, and you are quite right, this is a big voice. I hear him and see him as clearly as I hear you and see you, and as I hear him there is an answer somewhere, that is beginning to emerge. You know what I think?

*E.H.* What?

*F.R.* I think that I must quit business. I don't know how and when but I must somehow find out and do something quite different. I am not that old yet that I cannot start some kind of training.

*E.H.* Training in what?

*F.R.* I am not sure at all but when he [i.e. the sage] said to me that I am afraid that I might become one of those dead men walking around, it is absolutely true. I need some form of training where I can be of use to people. I would not mind becoming a teacher or something. What you are doing is not exactly what I had in mind. I would somehow like to combine my organizing capacity with actual assistance to people. No, teaching would not do, I have to work this out.

*E.H.* All right. Give an answer then to the old man. How would you sum it up?

(There is a very long silence, after which he said:)

*F.R.* Shall I tell you or shall I tell him?

*E.H.* Tell him.

*F.R.* Well, it is clear that what I have got is a concern for people, experience in organizing, and a wish to be alive. From these few scattered thoughts I must begin to build some solid foundation.

(I replayed the tape for him and he listened very attentively, and then he said:)

*F.R.* Well, that's it. There is a decision in me. Now the question is how to go about it?

I shall reflect presently on the process and underlying principles of the dialogue, but before doing so perhaps yet another case illustration would be helpful. In this case I will simply record the patient's confrontation with his paraphant and will not describe the situation and circumstances of the patient, as some of these will be clear from the actual dialogue itself.

*Dialogue with Dr A (case 8)*
(Age 47, married, one child)
The interview took place in Canada.
(Dr A also is moving across a jungle towards a particular clearing.)

*Dr A* As I am moving towards the clearing, out from the jungle, after what I have said earlier I am convinced that I like my work very much. The ultimate question that I have been left with through my interviews with you, and also through the final summary of my scale, is: 'What have I got to offer to life?' This, then, is the question that I have to bear in mind, and this is the question to which I really need an answer.

*E.H.* Describe what you see.

*Dr A* Well, I see the surf, white foam, a very smooth beach.

(At this point Dr A begins to cry.)

*E.H.* Why are you so emotional?

*Dr A* It is the conflict of *who* I want to choose [i.e. as a paraphant]. My dad?

(Dr A is very deeply moved and for a little while he is trying to collect his thoughts and feelings.)

*Dr A* I see the surf, the foam, and a very smooth beach, the sand is dark brown at the edge of the water. I see a thatched hut, something I imagine exists in Hawaii. I see a man coming to the door of the hut, very old; he has a long beard, almost as you expect a shipwrecked person would have. I hear the surf. He stands there and looks at me. I walk up to him very slowly.

I can't go any further.

*E.H.* You will have to ask him sooner or later your question, what have you to offer to life?

*Dr A* Well, I go up and just say to him: 'What do I have to offer . . . '

(Dr A again cries.)

. . . he comes outside the hut and we sit down together. The sage says to me: 'It took you a long time'.

(Some silence and the patient is still very emotional)

I say to the sage: 'You care for people; you understand their problems. You care. You understand them, the problems. I get the feeling that people can understand from you and you can understand from them.

(Again silence and several long sighs)

*E.H.* So you are engaged in conversation with this old man. How do you feel at this point of time?

*Dr A* I am very moved. I don't know, I just feel.

*E.H.* Is it a good feeling?

*Dr A* Almost. It is in between. Neither good nor bad. Just feelings.

*E.H.* Try to formulate your question; because if you do not ask the question you will not get an answer.

*Dr A* O.K. So we are sitting there. He is a kindly man, and I ask him: 'What do I have to offer?' And he says: 'You have the ability to take thought, you have philosophical insights, and can present them to people in the way they can understand and feel. You yourself are not a first-rate thinker but you can, with a lot of work, co-ordinate other people's thinking so that in turn people can take out of this the things that are relevant to their lives.'

*E.H.* In what kind of setting is it that you could use this ability? Look now into the future.

*Dr A* The old man says to me: 'Take this ability and use it. One place where you can use it is the church. Another place would be an educational setting, although you do not have confidence in that area because you feel that there you would have to be the pure scholar and you do not have confidence in yourself in that area. But there is room for what you have in an educational setting.' What about other areas?

*E.H.* Don't think it out; ask him, because he knows!

(For the first time the patient laughs)

*Dr A* Are there other places? Because this to me depends on the situation being right. Are there other areas that I can move into - areas where I don't have to wait for the system to approve me or say 'O.K. we can hire you'? I draw a blank here.

*E.H.* So you don't get an answer to that one.

*Dr A* No, I don't get an answer to that one.

*E.H.* It seems to me that you received an answer to the question of what you have got, but you haven't received an answer to the question, where you can use this. Now ask him what it is that you have not got.

*Dr A* You [addressing the old man] told me what I have got and what I can do. What *don't* I have? The old man replies to me: 'I mentioned one thing — you don't have confidence in being creative. Probably you are not.'

(Silence)

'You also don't seem to have the confidence at this point to promote your own self . . . . ' I get lost.

*E.H.* That you got lost . . . this is how we have started, but don't worry about it too much.

(At this point the patient listens back on the tape to what has been experienced so far. He listens carefully and during the process he begins to relax as he sits, and when he begins to speak his voice has changed completely; the uncertainty has gone from his voice; the tears have stopped and he now quite deliberately says:)

*Dr A* For reasons which I cannot clearly explain my whole problem seems to be around the question of control.

*E.H.* The issue that concerns you is something to do with control?

*Dr A* I think so. There are many things in this area that frustrate me. It seems to me that there is something left out of that word [i.e. control]. I can't take the statement any further just now.

(His voice has now a controlled, clear and logical quality. Then a little later:)

You can take the word in the Bible sense, self-control, controlling others. But is there more here that you see but that I cannot see? It is clear to me now that the issue is that of control, being domineered or something like that. It seems to me that I do not accept too well. I have been aware of it before, but I can see that problems have arisen around this word. I was aware of these things but I was not able to pin this down to one thing.

*E.H.* The issue is not what you have become aware of . . . you know . . .

*Dr A* It is what I can do with it.

*E.H.* We will leave it at that for the moment and then we shall come back to it before the afternoon is out.

(Again, having listened to this part of our encounter on the tape, he says:)

*Dr A* How far ahead I am now from where we began! I did not, for example, realize until now that one of my ambitions was really possibly to teach, because I have questioned my intellectual ability. It becomes now more clear that I must have lived with this somehow without spelling it out clearly to myself. The issue, however, is that in order to achieve this ambition I have to become more free in my relationships with people outside this possible teaching situation. This lack of self-confidence about my intellectual ability is really very silly if you come to think of it, because when I was sixteen I was not doing that badly in school — then somehow, comparing myself with others, I ran away with the idea that I was not the intellectual type. I somehow, even as a young man, always felt that intellectual achievement was not something for myself but was something that others had decided for me. So I could not feel that I was 'clever' for my own sake but only as I saw others reacting to me. It is for this reason that any kind of supervision, or other people's decisions as to whether or not I should be hired, makes me resentful, because I am not dependent on my own intellectual ability but rather on them.

So it is control and relationship. I am not as far along, for example, in my relationship to Maureen [his wife] as I would like to be. I would like to be remarried now to her and start afresh from what I know now, but that of course is impossible.

*E.H.* How old are you?

*Dr A* Forty-seven. If I were married again I would give to my marriage different priorities. But I feel quite hopeful for the future. Although I now feel, having said what I have said, more hopeful about my work situation, because of the mistakes I have made with Maureen I wish I could feel more hopeful with her.

On the whole life has meaning for me and I look forward to travelling more than I have been able to do in the past. I have given up so many things in order to have an education, which means in this process I now feel that I have missed out on some things. Yet I can't complain because life has given me a great deal.

(At this point of time he is taking out of his file his scale which he did on a previous occasion.)

I always felt so much inhibited in expressing myself. My relationship with my father [looks at the scale] was characterized by being dominated by him. He was kind of dictatorial. So I have kept a lot of my feelings to myself. I did not quite know how to handle things in relationship to myself. I think that life is giving me increasingly more scope for self-expression, and as I am not seeing him that often my relationship with my father is much better, although of course he is now quite old. I have a sister and a step-brother; I did not know that I had a step-brother until quite late, and finding this out was quite a shock.

Dad was married before and I did not know for a long time that he was. He did not know that he had another son. He did not discover it until much later. The discovery of this step-brother added to my shyness and to my becoming more and more reserved. Now I wish I could spend more time with my brother but he is living in Australia. As I have always had a difficulty about making friends, I had hoped that this newly-discovered brother would be one.

Really, to sum up, had I had a better relationship with my father I would not have been so isolated and alone, and perhaps would not have questioned the kind of things that throughout this afternoon I have been questioning, that is to say my intellectual ability. But if I now look at everything it seems that, despite the difficulties, things have worked out quite well for me. So to the question that I have put originally: What can I offer to life? Although I am not certain, and I am far from being able to make up a proper plan, by testing out my relationships, starting with Maureen and moving on to other people, and perhaps visiting my step-brother in Australia to spend some more time with him, I could move more and more by gaining confidence towards some form of teaching in my profession. But whether or not I would achieve this does not depend entirely on me. A few years more will have to be spent not only on brushing up what I know but also learning new things. If Maureen is willing to make some sacrifices I might have an opportunity to do something useful, not that I think that so far I have been useless.

In Case 5 (Eva), the patient, after mourning her husband and having gone through a reactive depression, had begun to ask herself whether she had done with her life what she was *capable* of doing. She also asked the age-old question of man: whether she could do something more meaningful? It was around this inner theme of being capable and meaningful that she had begun to reconstruct the apparently broken pieces of her life. It is doubtful whether in Eva's case her answer could have come from looking backwards into the past and unravelling the various causative factors that had led to the present. Had she known such explanations it is still questionable whether these would have added up to the examination of her capabilities and meaning. Although of course such hypothetical questions are of little use, it seems to me that such techniques which aim to increase insight and understanding in relation to the past, however *mind-relieving* they may be, certainly do not necessarily relieve the increasingly urgent issues that the psyche poses; i.e., what is the meaning and the purpose of it all? And here, it seems, we are confronted with two interrelated issues, i.e. that of the mind and that which Carl Gustav Jung calls the psyche.

The ancient Hebrews gave an even more appropriate word to this inner meaning. They called it *Ruah*. This Ruah, according to religious beliefs, is the spirit that God put in man during the days of the creation. It was that that differentiated man from other living beings, and appeared to be a real factor towards the search for a fuller life. It is in that sense that this word is used here, i.e. the search for purpose and meaning. The Ruah includes the magic of childhood, a dressing-gown which begins to be filled with life and turns into a fairy and a witch. It is the Ruah that needs to become the paraphant so that it is not just a vague and woolly feeling but something that can be stated, communicated with; something capable of giving answers to questions.

As it was the first occasion on which I became aware of the journey that Eva (and after her, so many others) was capable of making, I had to recognize that some diseases of the mind can also be connected with an attempt to deny the existence of this Ruah in man. It appears that when Eva had begun to be in touch with the fairy and the witch, a metamorphosis had occurred in her own life, and this great change was expressed in her case through artistic means. In short, she had liberated in herself that Ruah, formulated it, and organized it into a paraphant.

In Case 6 (Norman) the dialogue did not move to the same kind of dimensions. It was not (at least as manifestly expressed) a problem of meaning and purpose, but rather one that related to a middle-aged man's inability to get promotion which *he* considered was his due. During this process, he found himself face to face with that Greek sage who turned away from him and did not answer. 'He just sits there and turns his back on me.'

This may very well be an important lesson as to the differentiation between treatment of the mind and the activation of the Ruah. It may very well mean (although I am not sure of this) that the Ruah can be activated, and a true paraphant can be evoked, only if one has solved those problems that are concerned with the *reality* of existence rather than with the *meaning* of it. It may very well be that the Ruah cannot and will not allow itself to be made into a paraphant if (quoting Norman) 'I cannot *provoke* an answer'. It is almost certain that man cannot provoke a paraphant. It appears that Norman could have received an answer only had he been able to solve through other methods (social functioning or otherwise) some of his basic problems, not only in relation to promotion but also to his marriage.

In Case 7 (F.R.) the situation is not unlike that of the case of Eva. This forty-year-old man had lost his dreams and what he tried to do through the dialogue was to regain those dreams and to transform them, or at least some aspect of them, into reality.

He says: 'The funny thing is that the whole thing is so clear . . . . He [the paraphant] is very friendly and he knows why I am there . . . . I hear him and see him as clearly as I hear you and see you, and as I hear him, there is an answer somewhere that is beginning to emerge . . . .' And at the end: 'There is a decision in me. Now, the question is how to go about it?'

Here we find all the important ingredients of a successful dialogue. 'The whole thing is clear' - and there is surprise that this should be so. We have so much de-conditioned ourselves from believing in the magical quality of life that when we are face to face with it we think it smacks of a miracle. However, once having experienced the 'miracle', it stays put; one begins to seek beyond the walls of the consulting-room and many find it in day-to-day living.

There is one further aspect of the dialogue which should be covered here and that is the conscious projection of the symptom, or some aspect of it, on to the external world. Gestalt psychologists have used somewhat similar techniques. The symptom is 'personified' so that the patient can have a conversation with it, in which case the paraphant becomes the symptom itself. It often advises the patient as to its meaning and as to how it can be used by the patient in a more positive way, so that its destructive nature may become constructive.

A man of fifty-eight, a bank manager, had gone through a rather stressful period with a great deal of real anxiety because of circumstances beyond his control. He weathered the storm well until one morning when on getting dressed he had a 'terrifying dizzy spell' and he fell. This was coupled with severe palpitations and 'cold sweat'. Terrified that he had had a stroke or a heart attack, he called a doctor, but examination showed that nothing was wrong with him physically.

Then he came to see me. My interviews with him took place several weeks after his first attack, which was followed by others which were similar, and he now complained of a continuing 'swimmy feeling' which caused him grave anxiety. I went through the various aspects of the social functioning method with him but we did not seem to get anywhere. Nothing seemed to help him. He could not get through the dialogue because it seemed that he lacked creative imagination, so I finally decided to try to get him to 'personify' his symptom and to consciously project it on to a chair. In other words his main complaint, dizziness, was now sitting in front of him and facing him. He described the symptom as a continuous spinning, lightening-like shape, reddish in colour, the size of a man. I asked him to get in touch with this symptom and inquire as to its origin. He did not seem surprised when 'the symptom' answered him. It said that it was to do with a personal decision which he, the patient, was unable to make and which was upsetting his sense of balance. Further conversation with the symptom revealed some possible solutions as to how he might come to a satisfactory decision and so bring his conflict to an end. At the end of the interview, the patient saw the symptom lift from the chair, move towards the window and evaporate into space. Although he still felt uneasy, the dizzy feeling left the patient from then on, never to return.

## Summary notes on the dialogue

In order to bring about a successful dialogue, there are a number of points to be taken into consideration.
1) The dialogue cannot be a *starting point* of treatment.
2) The patient must have experienced himself through the

other methods described before (initial interview, scale, statement).

3) The patient's 'main emerging theme' has to do with meaning and purpose (or the lack of these).

4) On the whole, the patient must feel that life so far was worth the struggle (see question 5 on the synthesis index of the scale).

5) The patient must not be afraid of imagination, or consider imagination to be inferior to rationality. (In Case 6 Norman said: ' . . . this is a silly game . . . . '.)

6) The patient must not have lost the wish or the capacity for play (in the child's sense).

# 7 Group Treatment

The methods described so far have some application to the treatment not only of individuals but also of groups. The primary group, the family, can benefit particularly by the processes described here as such processes allow marital partners, for example, to communicate with each other and to appreciate the experiences of the other. Family treatment may be divided into two somewhat interconnected practices: that used with marital partners and that used with the whole family. There may be an additional aspect of this treatment method that is being used in premarital counselling, but as this is somewhat similar to the methods used with marital partners, the latter will be described.

### Marital counselling

Although no hard and fast rules can be applied to the method used with marital partners, experience so far has shown that it is advisable in the first instance to see the partners separately both for the initial interview and for the application of the scale. This procedure allows the two individuals to:

1) have a peer-relationship with the therapist;
2) have the opportunity to state, and to reflect on, the satisfactions and frustrations of his/her own life;
3) after such reflection, formulate the decision as to whether or not such a recording of self-observation, or any part of such recording, should be shared with the partner;
4) to learn from personal experience that some confirmation of past and present satisfactions and frustrations may not only be stated but may also be meaningful: through the respect that the therapist will show to the individual patient, he/she may begin to be able to respect the as-yet unheard but stated experiences of the partner.
5) Such perception, even at this stage, may change the emphasis of human problems so that these are viewed from a point of view of respect rather than blame.
6) If so far such patterns of observations and feelings have

appeared in the individual patient, it is more than likely that similar attitudes of respect will prevail when each shares the other's experience by listening to the recorded statements, reflections and tentative conclusions.

I would like to emphasize, however, that if the break between marital partners has already occurred to such an extent that they are capable of stating and observing only the negative aspects of their marital relationship, the confrontation will have little usefulness and should be avoided. Marriages that are breaking can perhaps be saved, not so those that are already broken. In short, there must be *some* wish to save the marriage. At no time do I impose my will on the patient. This has been said and emphasized before. The same applies to the issue of bringing partners together with a view to making such a meeting a truly sharing experience. It is not, therefore, *my* judgement, opinion or decision that ultimately will decide the future course of action; this is left entirely to the two people concerned. If either of them is unwilling, then I cannot insist that such a meeting should take place.

After the initial interviews and the responses to the scale, the husband and wife may be brought together, provided that they are in full agreement to do so. The process of this combined interview may be as follows.

1) During the first of such combined sessions the participants may wish to share the conclusions and their recorded reflections.

2) They may wish, in turn, to listen to the total recordings or to some part of these.

3) They may wish, either at this interview or during later interviews, to share their scale and the conclusions and the details of it with each other.

4) Each may then begin to ask questions, and/or generally make comments on their perception of what each has heard. At the same time, each can state his own perceptions.

5) The therapist will from time to time try to sum up what he has understood the partners to have said.

6) He will then help the partners individually, and later on *together,* to agree at least on what has been stated so far.

7) Such combined statements may be separately recorded.

8) At the end of the session the partners will listen to the combined summary statements and will be asked to formulate a synthesis of these.

9) They will both be asked to contemplate the summary statements and reflect on what action might follow.

As the process of interviewing has been described in previous chapters, there appears to be no need to repeat these methods in relation to marital counselling or treatment. The important aspect here is that although marital partners may have said to each other the kind of things that come forth during the combined interview, they have probably not experienced the safety and the right to statement to the degree that now becomes a possibility. While, of course, blame, accusation and bitterness may still be projected on to one another, the therapist's function is to point out that these subjective perceptions of each individual should be, or at least should be attempted to be, respected. In a sense, the therapist is asking the partners to enter into a kind of contract during the period of the combined session, during which they will preserve the same right and respect to individual experience in each other as he, the therapist, has given during previous sessions to the partners. Experience has shown that often, but not of course invariably, such communication patterns are of considerable therapeutic value. Marital partners often say: 'I can now see his/her point of view *differently*'. If the therapist attempts to clarify the nature of the difference, more often than not the partners will observe that they are not entirely responsible for the other's misfortunes, nor are they clear as to where their responsibility does in fact begin.

The following briefly recorded situation provides an example of this.

The husband, aged twenty-eight, an unskilled worker who was periodically unemployed, accused his wife, aged twenty-four, of not trusting him. In fact he thought that his wife's perception of him was that he was capable of becoming a thief during his periods of unemployment. She wore a little gold cross around her neck and apart from the engagement and wedding rings she had one or two non-expensive pieces of fancy jewellery. Each night she hid her prized possessions, as she thought her husband would take them away from her. The young man was extremely angry with her and told her that he had never taken anything in his life. How could he even think of doing such a thing to his wife whom he loved? The usual reply from the wife was that: ' . . . all men, when in a tight corner, would steal and worse'. On such occasions the husband would leave her and drink excessively at a nearby bar and return home half drunk. On one occasion he insisted in such a half-drunken state that his wife forthwith produce her 'bloody rubbish' (referring to her prized possessions). When she was unwilling to do so he physically attacked her.

Although both husband and wife had had little education, he was soon able to understand when he heard on the tape his wife's account of her childhood experiences on the scale's primary family section. He heard her saying on the tape that her father used to take her mother's possessions and either pawn or sell them. She, in turn, was deeply impressed by the fact that it was his impotent rage that drove him to drinking, and, as she put it, 'I could never fancy that it was because he really loves me'.

It is this kind of communication in a dimension hitherto not experienced that makes it possible for partners to understand how far, in this instance, past experiences had influenced the young woman to project the image of the thief-father on to an innocent husband. The wife understood in a way she had not before done so, how much this must have hurt her young husband. No interpretation whatsoever was given by the therapist.

When patients present themselves with personal problems that are apparently related or unrelated to the marital situation, I find it advisable to establish how far such problems do exist. Experience has shown that a number of patients may 'offer' psychogenic or psychosomatic syndromes. When these are but the visible part of the iceberg, direct questions (or even indirect ones) may not reveal the true nature of the inter-personal conflicts between partners.

During 1970 I worked out a 'social responsibility scale' (SR scale) which is at present in an embryonic form and needs a great deal of validation. The initial pilot studies, however, that I have personally carried out with a number of patients, indicate that this scale, used in combination with the other scale, the HSSF, may have some merit. The SR scale is given to the partner and/or the children of whomever is identified as the patient. The patient's permission is sought after the initial interview to enable the therapist to have a diagnostic picture as to the marital and/or family functioning. The SR scale has, so far, been self-administered by the patient's husband and/or wife or family and returned to the therapist for diagnostic evaluation. This scale tries to evaluate the subjective perception of individuals in the patient's family as to their feelings and attitude towards the patient. It consists, so far, of twenty-five questions, as had the HSSF in its initial stages. These are aimed at evaluating the way in which members of the family perceive the patient's responsibility towards them in five distinctive areas. The five areas of responsibility are:

1) provision;
2) emotional nature;
3) reliability;
4) personality;
5) synthesis.

Although at this point validation is lacking as to the reliability of the SR scale, particularly if used in connection with the HSSF, one could tentatively presume that at least some connections do exist.

A number of permutations now become possible. Let us assume that the patient's subjective perceptions of his satisfactions on the HSSF are high and, for argument's sake, that the subjective perceptions of the wife on the SR scale are low. Because of the similarity of the areas, one would expect that the different patterns of score responses will indicate different subjective perceptions, and in consequence a tentative diagnosis of marital stress may be made. It is, for example, quite conceivable that the subjective perception of a man's financial satisfactions could be high and the wife's subjective perception of her husband's financial responsibility and attitude towards her low. This kind of score pattern would indicate that the husband either consciously or unconsciously distorts the truth or that the wife does so. Whatever the reason for such conflicts may be, such different patterns of subjective perceptions must indicate at least one area of disagreement.

The situation, of course, becomes more complicated if such contradictions between the HSSF (scored by the patient) and the SR scale (in this instance scored by the wife) show a multiple of conflict situations. If one partner, for example, states that he/she is experiencing a high level of sexual satisfaction while the other partner complains of frustration, then there is no question but that conflicts do exist. In this kind of situation, the therapist may seek permission from the wife (who had filled out the relevant answers on the SR scale) to involve her in some way in the treatment situation, and in consequence to encourage the partners to use the scale responses for communication purposes.

If there are adolescent children in the family, the SR scale may give the therapist some guidance as to who in the family suffers most and/or what kind of inter-personal problems exist in the total family situation. Experience has also shown that husband and wife may be quite happy *with each other,* to the exclusion of a child or children. Conversely, it is quite possible that the children may have high satisfaction ratings to the exclusion of either father and/or mother, although this latter situation is somewhat rare.

One weakness of individually-centred therapy has been that other members of the family are not receiving help simultaneously. The use of the SR scale with members of a family gives the therapist a clue as to the need for involving some or all members of the family in treatment. It is sometimes possible (depending on the nature of problems presented by the family group) for the therapist to undertake the treatment of the entire family or, if it is advisable, to involve another therapist. Such work has been undertaken by two therapists attending marital partners at the former Family Discussion Bureau of the Tavistock Institute of Human Relations, London (now the Institute of Marital Studies).

Although there is as yet weak evidence to support this, it is feasible that it would be possible, by using the HSSF and the SR scale, to evaluate the 'mean' functioning of the total family. This could be of considerable relevance to evaluation and treatment. Further studies will undoubtedly be in this direction.

## Group treatment

Social functioning method can be used with groups as well as with individuals and families. Group composition may vary from alcoholics to delinquents and some work has already been done (see section in appendix on research and experiments). Although no hard and fast rules may be made, some principles worthy of statement do emerge.

In group treatment it is advisable for the therapist to have at least two sessions with members of the group individually. These sessions include the initial interview and the use of the scale as a treatment instrument. During these sessions the emerging peer-relationship may help the individual patient to fit into the group later and to develop a sense of respect towards his/her own problems and those of other members of the group. The mutual trust between therapist and patient should help to achieve this.

Therapeutic groups in social functioning usually have eight members including the therapist. Having all gone through the sharing experience with the group co-ordinator, they will be more inclined to share their scale profiles with each other within the group.

A member of the group is asked to comment on his/her scale responses, and the other members are asked to reflect on their own thoughts and feelings, not in relation to what they have heard from the group member but in regard to how this applies to them individually. In short, members of the group are entering into a kind of agreement not to *advise* each other but rather to share their own experiences in connection with what the individual member's reaction to his/her scale response may trigger off in themselves.

As the permutation possibilities are so wide, it is impossible that any member of the group will have identical score patterns with another member. Although the group has been formed because there is some commonalty of problems, the nature of these as revealed by the score patterns is highly individual. In consequence, members of the group have different subjective experiences, positive or negative, in connection with what they are reacting to as one of the group conveys his/her own meaning. There will be some who have been able to deal successfully with some aspects where others may have failed. The sharing of such positive and negative reactions may be highly therapeutic both for individuals and for the group as a whole.

The therapist's or group co-ordinator's function is to record from time to time the synthesis or summary of what has been said and, at the end of the interview, to share the totality of such summaries with the group. Each time the group is asked to make further comments on such summaries and to interpret in relation to themselves any conclusions they may have as to what they have learned from the group. Whatever other function the group may have, one of its most relevant features is that in their totality the group members represent a vast reservoir of human experience. Such experience, collected by the group co-ordinator and shared with the group, helps the process of self-actualization.

Miss J. L. Dighton worked with groups for many years and eventually she began to include the methods described here in her group work practice. One extremely interesting aspect of her work was the relatively fast reaction of some delinquent boys to the notion of using one's frustrations creatively. Also, it was very interesting that in her group experimentation, when working with the scale 'those who found it easy were invited to help the dullards'. Miss Dighton's work with groups of psychotics has begun only recently (1970), and it will be interesting to see whether social functioning will have a place in such a helping process.

The Rev. David Savill (a Church of England clergyman) has used the scale with various groups in his parish. These have included pre-marriage groups as well as various discussion groups. He found that social functioning methodology had serious relevance to the Christian community and he feels that such methods might revive and revitalize the work of the church.

Apart from these pioneering groups, there are many other professional workers who have used some social functioning methods with groups.

The difference between social functioning and other forms

of group therapy is comparable to the difference between these types of therapy in the treatment of individuals. Group members may interpret *their own* internal or external life patterns, but they may not interpret each other's, nor would they be encouraged to advise each other in the ordinary sense of the word. People do not seem to learn from advice, but they need to find supporting individuals inside and outside treatment who, by sharing their own life experiences frankly and honestly, can help to activate a more balanced view of the self. One can learn only from one's own experiences, and thus in a sense treatment and learning are very much interconnected.

# 8 Educational Counselling

Learning begins with the exploration of the self. The first such achievements, in the first months and years of childhood, are concerned with the control over the body, the use of hands, mouth, legs, etc. There is no greater achievement for the child than to be able to *do* something and, by repetition, to gain knowledge of and mastery over his actions. Some children may need encouragement and stimuli while others may begin such explorations without much outside influence. *The child learns because he wants to learn.*

Problems arise later when others, in the adult world, define the borders of learning. Imagination and learning go hand in hand initially, and imaginative teachers can achieve remarkable success with dull children because the emphasis is on imagination and not necessarily on intellectual achievement. This chapter will be concerned mainly with the educational processes of the post-adolescent youngster, i.e. with those who enter higher education establishments, colleges and universities. However, many patterns that apply to the more mature student will also apply to the less mature. Although in the Hounslow Project (work done to validate the scale) some attempts were made to work with younger age groups (even if only for a short period), most of my own experience has been with university students and with groups of adults in programmes of further or continuing education.

The basic question of higher education revolves around the problem of who should decide what should be taught and also how this knowledge should be absorbed by the student. Many students develop a conscious or unconscious resistance to learning when they are confronted by a rigid syllabus where it is not very clear how far the material to be learned is of relevance to them and when they feel unsure about whether or not they can absorb the knowledge into their own experience.

Speaking of my own sphere, of those who wish to work directly with people, I often wonder whether we have not put the cart before the horse? This may easily apply to other forms of professional disciplines. It appears that available social work knowledge may be meaningful to the student only if he truly wishes to explore the spectrum himself and not if it is simply superimposed on him. In order to enable the student to *wish to learn,* a particular tutorial system which could help with the formulation of questions and then with answers, might be helpful..

The young student entering social work may not be sure whether his chosen field is the right one. This, by the way, also applies to many students who have left high school or secondary school. Often the choice is haphazard, and lack of experience, confusion about one's abilities or the inability to relate inner problems to the outer world may mean that the young man or woman chooses a profession framework that is inappropriate for him or her. The first aim of higher education should be an exploration of how the inner self can relate to the outer. There should be at least a year in which expressed intentions are taken, both by the student and by the teachers, with a 'pinch of salt'. Instead of bombarding the young college or university student with a set syllabus, there should be an intensive and imaginative exploration of his gifts, abilities, aspirations and future intentions. The tutorial system might be helpful, and in my experience often is, in achieving some clarification.

There are many ways and techniques by which this can be done, but the young person needs to have access to an experienced teacher who, in the first instance, would see such candidates in small groups. Such a tutor, apart from being skilled in group methodology not unlike that described under group treatment (chapter 7), also should in my opinion be a 'general practitioner of education'. Whether his basic training is in art, literature or science, the teacher should have training in specific group educational processes.

What I am describing here is only one of the many possibilities of group educational counselling, and modifications and alterations of this methodology may be as numerous as the individual tutors who undertake the training of such groups. The groups should be small, between seven to eleven students. Initially, the topic of discussion must relate to a number of questions that the students may put:

   1)   in relation to the tentatively chosen field;

2) whether or not their past experience and interest enables them to fit into that field.

One member of the group may formulate a question, 'What is social work?' The other members of the group would then respond with what their understanding of social work is. There is an initial understanding that a question that has been posed by one of the group members does not need an authoritative answer, but rather that each student should express his or her understanding of what the question means to himself or herself. Answers, therefore, are not 'advice' to the questioner but rather an expression of one's own understanding of the question.

The task of the group tutor will be seen to be manifold
1) He will state the nature of the 'contract' under which the tutorial group would operate, i.e. that questions have to be formulated by individual members and that the answers to such questions are, in fact, monologues by individuals as to their own understanding of what that question means to them.
2) The group tutor will act as a synthesizer. From time to time he will sum up the essence of what has been said so far and return to the questioner for his reactions to what he has heard. He will also ask the questioner to react as to his feelings, whether he feels comfortable or otherwise with what has been said so far.
3) The group tutor can supply factual information as to the question raised (what is social work?) and may suggest some preliminary reading on this subject.
4) The tutor will see to it that before a further question is asked, which often arises from a discussion, the questioner is fully satisfied with reactions received.
5) Further questions can then be formed and answered in a somewhat similar fashion.

Apart from written material, imaginative videotape presentations would be adaptable to group tutorials. It is important that such visual presentations should not be further discussions or lectures but should be action-orientated. For example, groups of students may wish to view experienced social workers in action in various settings of social work practice. Afterwards further tutorials could, and no doubt would, deal with some of the reactions and questions that arise from the observation of this videotape material. Such videotape material could also include interviews with social workers about the satisfactions and frustrations, problems and solutions in relation to their professional work. It should also be available to cover a wide field of settings in which students are likely to be working, i.e. factories, offices, mines, oil plants, etc. For example, if the students have been observing a social worker interview a postman, some videotape material could be available about the life, working and private, of postmen. If during the videotape presentation the postman should refer, say, to inadequate working conditions, subsequent tutorials might deal with the trade union aspects of the postman's dilemma and bring into the tutorial knowledgeable people (professors or others) on this subject.

In short, one basic question, for example 'What is social work?', may lead far and wide; and the various components, as one pattern leads to another, will make the whole issue of learning a creative and interesting one. Learning then evolves through the interest of individual students. There will be students who will be less interested in, say, the trade union aspects of the postman's dilemma than in his hobbies or interests. Further videotape materials should then be available to deal with a wide field of leisure activities, and teachers and others who would be able to discuss these aspects with the students could be brought into the group.

In time, while the original tutor would retain the original group, other tutorial sessions - special interest groups - would be formed under other tutors. Through such methodologies and practices, individual students would have a clearer idea of whether they would wish to pursue their study in social work or would rather move into some other field. If three students out of eight, for example, would be led to recognize that their ability lay not in direct work with people but in literature, art, or for that matter engineering, then they should have access to group advisers who would similarly explore their questions in these alternative fields and supply answers in a similar manner as described above.

The tutorial methods described in relation to the under-graduates can also be applied with some modification to the curriculum of undergraduate study *after* the student has made his final choice. It would also be applicable to the graduate courses. The following reconstruction of an actual group tutorial is presented here with a view to describing the process, the role of the group tutor and the agreement that the various group members enter into in order to achieve a successful tutorial session. The group consisted of four men and three women plus myself as group tutor. There was also another faculty member in attendance who, as will be seen later, had a specific task of recording the synthesis or sum-maries of what had been said by the various group members. In total, this particular group consisted of nine people. For simplicity's sake I shall refer to myself as group tutor 1, to my colleague as group tutor 2, and to the students as group member A, B, C, etc.

*Group tutor 1* The purpose of the exercise is to clarify some of our questions in relation to the subject you have been studying for the last few months, social functioning. You have been attending lectures and have had the opportunity to experience individually with me the process of interviewing and the use of the scale of social functioning [HSSF scale], both as a diagnostic instrument and as a treatment device. You have been reading available material on this subject, and yet there are a number of questions that still have not been answered and some-how you have had little chance to integrate your knowledge, pragmatic as well as emotional.

In order to facilitate a process of integration, questions have to be formulated as clearly as possible before answers can be given. The com-position and interest of the group defines the subject matter under discussion. If this were a group whose main interest was to co-ordinate and integrate their knowledge in relation, say, to various forms of social legislation and its relevance to practice, then this would define the kinds of questions and answers that would emerge. To be brief, we must enter into a kind of agreement that, for the next hour and a half, we use a rather disciplined way of coping with questions and answers. This discussion is necessary in order that we achieve a process of integration. I shall ask one of you to formulate a question as clearly and as precisely as you can. When that question is asked, we shall all test out whether we have understood that question. Having done so, the other members of the group will attempt to answer that question as if that were their own formulation. In other words, we shall attempt *to pose that question to ourselves* and answer it in as much detail and depth as we are capable of doing. In a sense, therefore, we are not attempting to tell the questioner what he or she is supposed to know, but simply what we know about that question. My colleague here [group tutor 2] has had training in encapsulating your answers so that at the end of our meeting we shall be able to reflect on what we have really said and then from that we can arrive at some conclusions. We cannot rest until the questioner is satisfied that his or her question has been fully answered. Finally, I do not wish to limit or interfere with the spontaneity of your reactions. It isn't necessary that individual group members, as they are formulating their answers, should give a lecture. What is necessary, however, is that every one of you can come in, at any time. It is also important that during this discussion we do not become involved with arguments, but rather with spelling out what we know. Let us proceed now and see what the questions will be. Would anyone like to start off?

There were a few moments of silence while the members of the group were trying to formulate their questions. During this time, one or two of the members asked for clarification as to the difference between answering someone else and posing the question to oneself. Having cleared these points, there was some silence for some time.

*Group member A* I have a question but I am not quite sure how to put this into words yet. I will try. We have learned that in social functioning the therapist's task is to help the patient to create a disciplined framework in which the patient can explore his life situation. There are, in fact, several thoughts occurring to me. How far is the relationship between the therapist and the patient important? What kind of relationship is this and would this method be applicable with patients that, say, are not able to look at themselves, or if they do, see only the negative aspects? I realize that this is not just one question, but many. Yet I cannot help feeling that there must be a great many patients with whom this method would not be successful and should not even be attempted. [Laughing] It is terribly difficult to put all these questions into one.

*Group tutor 1* I should be very grateful if, nevertheless, you could reflect on your questions and try to formulate one which may be a synthesis of all that you have asked. Don't worry, we have plenty of time.

There was a long silence and, as group members said later, they were rather eager at that point to *help* the questioner, but according to our agreement this was not permissible. It is always easier for somebody else to come to the rescue of some-body but it is very important that the questioner should have the right to struggle through in formulating what he or she wanted to ask. After a while, she said:

*Group member A* All right, my question must then be really: 'What is social functioning?'

*Group tutor 1* May I remind you all now to pose this question to yourselves as if this were your own question and try to answer it.

Again, some silence ensued. These silences are of great significance because they allow individuals to reflect on the question.

*Group member B* To me, social functioning first of all is a philosophy, and it seems to me that unless I identify myself, or, let me put it this way, unless I recognize having my own [philosophy], I couldn't possibly move on to help people help themselves. Now, what is that philosophy? [Brief silence] I think, basically, it is a belief or trust - yes, trust is a better word - that the patient is able and capable of arriving at his own solution. I think that man has got more in him than we often appreciate. I really believe that, given the opportunity and choice, he would rather choose satisfactory solutions than destructive ones.

*Group member C* I am a little bothered because I too am groping with this question of philosophy. Now you, Professor, have gone through certain awful experiences which I haven't gone through and, while I appreciate that these experiences left you with an ultimate trust in human beings, I am not sure that I have that.

*Group tutor 1* Let me see, in response to the original question, what this question regarding philosophy means to me. I have experienced man at his worst while I was in German concentration camps, and after that experience I was left with very great doubts. I remember that after the war when I returned home and found no one from my family alive, I went through a very severe depression. Eventually, somehow, somewhere, a choice presented itself to me. It wasn't as simple as I am making out now, nor do I understand fully how the decision regarding those choices came about. What happened was that when I realized the loneliness and, in some way, the hopelessness that surrounded me within and outside, I could easily have killed myself; I could easily have turned against others - and former Nazis could easily have been a socially acceptable target - or I could, as I did, begin to think that I might as well find out something about the human situation and, instead of creating wounds within myself or others, try to heal those wounds. In fact, to me, the philosophy basically consists of a choice and, somehow, the ability to make that choice. So then we all, irrespective of who we are, are faced constantly with such choices between constructive and destructive paths and, I suppose, our humanity consists of making a positive choice rather than a negative one.

*Group member D* Having listened to what has been said and also trying to answer the original question of what is social functioning, it seems to me that if man knows the choices that are available to him and if he trusts the therapist who treats the patient as an equal human being, then it is easier perhaps to make a constructive choice. But while, philosophically, I would agree with this, I am not sure whether invariably this would work with all people. What comes to my mind, for example, is someone who cannot make a choice. Someone completely paralysed or deeply depressed. It seems to me then that moving from the philosophic to the actual practice, we may have to make the choices clearer to him. So I don't think social functioning practice is that rigid; if people can use their self-determination, then we must do everything so that they can do so, but if they cannot, we can't just sit and wait for miracles to happen.

*Group member E* But what if people have a limited choice or no choice at all? If social functioning concerns itself with choosing between alternatives, then what if there is little or nothing to choose from? I have someone in mind, a case I am dealing with, a woman aged fifty-four, a former teacher who is suffering from an incurable disease. She knows and I know that she is going to die. What choice is there for her?

*Group member D* What comes to my mind, if she were my patient, is that we may at times have to substitute the word meaning for the word choice. Those who can choose may find meaning both in the present and in the future, but those who don't have such choice may still have meaning in the present and in the past. I wonder if one could explore this with her, not so much what is to be, but that which has been. If one allowed such a person the freedom of reviewing past actions, attitudes, thoughts and feelings, she may still come up with some kind of meaning, a philosophy, perhaps, or faith for the present. If this cannot be achieved, then the fact that someone is available and in tune with that person itself can be, at least, some help.

*Group member F* To me social functioning is a process of integration of experience. Because of the interaction between past and present and because such interaction is contained within a disciplined framework, such integration becomes possible and, in my limited experience, in a shorter space of time. There are in this method a number of significant factors that are present in other methods as well, except that in social functioning, perhaps, these are more circumscribed and precise. When I went through with our group tutor such actual experience of integration, it wasn't during the interview so much that I perceived a continuity running through my life, but rather later, when I had to cope with the number of episodes, some of them significant to my life. So it seems to me that this integration is a process which begins with the interview, perhaps began long before the interview, but the method reactivates such experience. My question is not whether we are dealing with a so-called new school of thought, but rather with a kind of integrated social work theory and methodology?

The preceding is only a brief abstraction from a tutorial session that lasted about an hour and a half. Most, if not all, members participated and at the end Group tutor 2 read her summaries so that the group could go away with something tangible. The summary might have read like the following:

*Group tutor 2* An agreement has been reached as to how these, or specifically this, tutorial session should be run. Questions have to be formulated and each individual poses this question to himself and answers it as if it were his own. The question that we have been dealing with here today is: 'What is social functioning?' It is a philosophy which the participants find true as being their own philosophy. Such philosophy arises from the synthesis of one's own experience. It deals with choice and expresses an hypothesis that if man is enabled to be alone with his life, he can evaluate and reflect upon it; such choices will be constructive rather than destructive. However, man must know the kind of choices that are open to him. There are some people, those for example who are depressed, who cannot make a choice. Whatever we do then is [done] to assist the patient to create a meaning from the past, the present or, hopefully, the future. We are left with the question as to whether this is a school of thought or an integrated social work theory and practice.

After such a discussion the students can react once more, and they often do react, to such summaries. Questions are often asked of the tutors who are present - in this case, for example, questions as to reading material on death and the dying. Some members may also wish to explore some aspect of the subject by reading from books or articles, perhaps of a literary kind that deals with the enjoyment of life. It is therefore the group tutor's task to supply such information and, if available, to refer them to videotape material already prepared or to encourage them to produce some such project on living and dying in audio or videotape themselves. Tutorials of this kind therefore do not define an *a priori* expectation of leading but rather supply a teaching aid as to the outcome of the process.

The kind of tutorial described above is only one of many possibilities, but all such tutorials will aim at integration of knowledge, insight, understanding and better practice.

# 9 Training Requirements

From experience it appears that it takes about sixty hours' training for people who are qualified in one of the helping professions to gain a *basic* knowledge of what has been described here as the practice of social functioning. In addition, they are required to undertake some personal interviews in order to supplement the theoretical knowledge by personal experience. At the basic training level four such interviews are often sufficient. At the more advanced training level more interviews are needed.

The syllabus of training can be obtained from one of the recognized centres of studies of social functioning, but it will be sufficient here to state that to date there appear to be four levels of competency.

First there is the *Licence-to-Use,* or *Certificate-to-Use,* level, which gives basic training in the interpretation of the scale.

This is usually followed by what we call *Associate Training,* which includes the interview methods, the use of the scale in interpretation *and* treatment, and the use of the statement (or Fragmenta Vitae). The entrance requirements to the Associate level in North America are professional social work (or some other professional qualification, i.e. psychology, psychiatry, etc.) with at least some years of experience in one's own field of competency. Usually the person admitted to such training has a master's degree or doctorate. In Britain the training requirements are dependent on full membership of a professional association (e.g. British Association of Social Workers), but the Licence-to-Use (LTU) or Certificate-to-Use (CTU) level is open to those who are working within the helping professions. In short, the training for Associates should consist of the basic LTU or CTU plus the use of the scale in treatment and the other interviewing methods. As I said earlier, personal interviews are part of this training. This is given by qualified lecturers in social functioning.

A *Lecturer* is a person who has a master's degree or other related degree and an Associate diploma. The training of Lecturers consists of about 180 hours of co-teaching under the direction of a qualified Lecturer. Such Lecturers have undergone a number of personal interviews and dialogues.

The requirement for *Fellow* is the MSW or related professional degree, an Associate diploma and an original contribution to social functioning theory and practice. Training for the Fellow practitioner level consists of six personal interviews (dialogue) and twenty training dialogues. Some of these are with patients and the data are evaluated by a Fellow.

Social functioning is used at present in several centres of studies in the USA, Canada, Britain and West Germany. The West German inquiries should be sent via Die Deutsche Verein. Others can be addressed to the Heimler Foundation, Elmhurst, High Street, Great Missenden, Bucks, England.

# 10 Interpreting the Scale

The utilization of the scale for treatment requires the competence of a qualified person within one of the 'helping professions' who has had some additional training in social functioning. Some level of competence in the interpretation of the scale can be extended to those who *de facto* are working with people, usually under the supervision of a fully trained person. Although the level of such interpretation would not reach that of a qualified and fully trained person, a number of such personnel, for example public health nurses, registered nurses and teachers, have found the scale useful in their day-to-day work.

This chapter deals with the interpretation of the scale and so the word 'interpreter' will be substituted for that of 'therapist'. Details of training in social functioning methodology have been dealt with in chapter 9.

Apart from its primary purpose as a treatment tool, the scale can also be used as a diagnostic instrument. Once the patient's responses are available it is possible for an interpreter to read and translate such responses, and to arrive at an assessment of the patient's stated self-perception as it related to the time when his scale was taken.

The interpretation of the scale for diagnostic purposes is in fact the interpreter's reading of the patient's responses and arriving at a conclusion that can be summed up thus: 'This is how the patient saw himself when his scale was taken'. As subjective responses often convey an objective reality, the skilled interpreter may then form his own conclusions as to the patient's situation. The use of the scale as a diagnostic instrument has been found useful as a sharing device among trained interpreters (i.e. in case conferences, transferring cases; on occasions when urgent action is required by someone other than the patient's own therapist; in supervisory roles and in professional teaching — in other words, in one of the 'helping professions').

Briefly, I would like to refresh the reader's memory about what the scale is all about, and then proceed to describe its diagnostic purpose. Finally I would like to explain how such interpretation can be arrived at.

The scale asks the patient fifty questions about his present life situation and five questions about how he perceives his past. These questions were arrived at through a process of elimination and through clinical experience and consideration, and cover the most relevant areas of life. Now, there may be questions other than the ones included in the scale which are, or could be, relevant, but the existing questions seem to enable the patient to associate freely to other relevant material, and to allow the therapist to make diagnostic sense of the patient's situation.

The permutation possibilities of fifty questions where the alternative answers can be 'yes', 'no' or 'perhaps' plus five questions in the synthesis, where one inquires about such issues as 'How far have you achieved your ambition in life?' and where the scoring moves in the feeling tone between 0 and 20, are mathematically astronomical: there could be eight thousand varieties per head of the population of Great Britain! This means that, provided the interpreter puts himself into the patient's shoes and reads the answers in the sense that the patient made them, he will in the first instance be able to state the patient's subjective perception of his situation. But at the same time it is possible for him, having identified himself with the patient and his perception, to look quite objectively at what he has said and to see whether or not he can make some kind of sense of this as an observer. After all, in the treatment situation the patient does the same thing. At first he states his answers and then eventually he interprets them. The difference between the patient's interpretation and that of the therapist is that the patient has access to his own life experiences while the therapist has not. Yet certain questions may be raised without such detailed knowledge, and certain answers (even if tentative) can be arrived at.

If I may give an example, in one of the financial sections for full and part-time employed the following questions are asked:

1) Do you live more comfortably than you did two years ago?

2) Are you able to save?

3) Do you feel at ease about spending?
4) Are you reasonably secure financially?
5) Do you feel financially secure?

Let us take now two individuals, A and B, who are answering such questions. The reader is reminded that 'yes' scores 4, 'perhaps' scores 2 and 'no', 0.

|  | Mr A | Mr B |
|---|---|---|
| 1) Do you live more comfortably than you did two years ago? | 4 | 0 |
| 2) Are you able to save? | 4 | 0 |
| 3) Do you feel at ease about spending? | 2 | 2 |
| 4) Are you reasonably secure financially? | 4 | 0 |
| 5) Do you feel financially secure? | 2 | 4 |

We have here ten responses, five from A and five from B. And now we shall try to interpret these.

The first thing we have in mind is that we cannot possibly know, as I have said in a previous chapter, the experiential meaning behind such a question as, for example, 'Do you live more comfortably than you did two years ago?', when Mr A says 'yes' and Mr B says 'no'. But when we are able to look through A's and B's answers, some questions present themselves which are the result of *pure logic*. Mr A in fact says this: 'I live more comfortably than I did two years ago; I am able to save; perhaps I feel easy about spending and perhaps not (I am really not certain about this). I am reasonably secure financially and perhaps I do feel financially secure (or at times), perhaps not.'

Now, we must ask, why is it that a man whose factual perception of his situation is positive does not feel certain about spending or about his financial security? Are there some *reality* factors here which are not stated within the given questions and answers? Or are the reality factors absent and is it simply that Mr A feels insecure for emotional reasons? I would of course not be able to come to any conclusion about Mr A's reply simply by the comparison and permutation and some seeming contradictions of his answers in this section. If, however, I have access not to five but to fifty-five such questions and answers, I would very soon be able not only to ask myself questions but to say that the insecurity that manifests itself in the financial area in at least two answers also manifests itself in some other areas. One could say therefore without much hesitation either that there are some relevant reality factors (because the uncertainty is not manifest in the other areas of his life) or that, if such patterns do exist in the other areas, then Mr A feels a. sense of insecurity for some unconscious or conscious reasons, or both.

Let me turn now to Mr B. Here the paradox of the answers becomes even more relevant, because his story regarding his finance is as follows: 'I am not living more comfortably than I did two years ago. I am not able to save. Perhaps I am at ease about spending and perhaps I am not (or sometimes). I am not reasonably secure financially but I *feel* financially secure.' The last answer definitely shows an illogical pattern from the point of view of the interpreter, because how can a man who describes himself as financially wanting and who states that all the facts about his finances are negative, *feel* financially secure? Also, how can such a person be uncertain about spending, or if he is, what does this mean?

Again, one cannot, simply by the comparison and permutation of such answers, arrive at any conclusion, but questions are arising in one's mind.

1) Are we dealing with someone who is capable of comprehending reality and the meaning of such reality?

2) Are we dealing with someone who is somewhat irresponsible in regard to his finances?

3) Who is the supplier of his finances, whatever they may be? Is it the State? Is it a parent? What?

Again, only questions are raised in one's mind; the answers cannot be forthcoming until one has had a chance of looking at his *other* answers. For example, if one notices that he answers the work section for 'unemployed', then one already knows a little more about what the possible answer could or would be. Once more, the answers in the other areas will also give an indication of the answers to our questions of 'responsible' or 'irresponsible', about ability to comprehend reality or not; and one can, after comparison and permutation of fifty-five questions, come out with an accurate diagnostic picture.

The question also must be raised, what happens if people are not honest in their answers? Experience shows that if three answers are given which are 'dishonest' this can be picked up through the kind of comparison and permutation that I have attempted to show above. This also applies to certain conditions of mental illness, when the answers are not distorted consciously but unconsciously, which may easily be the case (provided the other answers confirm this on the scale) in the case of Mr B.

In short, the interpreter's task is to look for consistencies and inconsistencies that are entirely logical, and while of course the internal story behind such patterns is unknown, yet with such wide interpretative possibilities quite accurate conclusions may be drawn.

Apart from internal consistencies and inconsistencies within the scale, the total score figures lend themselves to interpretation; in fact scale interpretations start with these. The interpretation of the score totals and general detailed drive for interpretation of the scale will be given in this chapter. Perhaps it is sufficient to say that the score totals are arrived at by adding up, in both the positive and negative indexes (i.e. the areas of satisfactions and frustrations), all the 4s, which as previously said are the definite answers and the 2s, the 'perhaps' and uncertain answers. Thus a score total on the positive index will look something like this: positive 72/84, mean score 78. Similarly, the negative index could be 8/26, mean score 17. The synthesis is obtained by simply adding the result on feeling tone - 88. The base positive 72 in the positive index is the result of eighteen 'yes' replies on the scale (18 x 4) and the upper 84 on the positive index means that there are six 'perhaps' answers (6 x 2 = 12, and 72 + 12 = 84).

On the negative index in this instance two 'yes' answers were given (- 8) and the difference between 26 and 8 means that there are nine uncertain answers (i.e. 9 x 2 = 18; 18 + 8 (the base negative) = 26).

The existing validation studies indicate that in Great Britain the mean for functioning is 72 to 79, with one-third to one-fifth scoring in the negative. The synthesis score is usually within 6 to 8 points of that of the positive. In the example that has been given, the interpretation would be something like this: 'This man functions within the norm but his frustrations and uncertainties are considerable, and although these seem to be contained, they cause him some tension which he is aware of.' This interpretation, of course, is not full, and a fuller one will be given on this particular case as well as on others later.

| | Totals | Mean score |
|---|---|---|
| Positive | 72/84 | 78 |
| Negative | 8/26 | 17 |
| Synthesis | – | 88 |

The interpretation of the scale for diagnostic purposes should be very systematic and disciplined, and following a standard procedure will help interpreters to achieve identical interpretations. I have found, and so have many of my colleagues who are now working with the scale, that the following steps are useful to bear in mind:

1) comment on the score totals;
2) comment on relationship between score totals;
3) comment on the internal consistencies and inconsistencies of positive or satisfaction area scores;
4) comment on the internal consistencies and inconsistencies of negative or frustration area scores;
5) comparison of consistencies and inconsistencies between positive, negative and synthesis indexes;
6) comment on synthesis index scores;
7) diagnosis, based on the above steps 1-6;
8) separation of such diagnosis from possible opinions of the interpreter.

**Comment on score totals**

| | Totals | Mean score |
|---|---|---|
| Positive | 72/84 | 78 |
| Negative | 8/26 | 17 |
| Synthesis | – | 88 |

Male, aged 44; married, 1 child aged 14, male; photographer.

The total positive index score (72/84: mean score 78) indicates that this man is well within the functioning range. The negative index total (8/26) with mean score of 17 confirms adequate functioning, as the negative index score should be within the range of 1/3 of the positive in the 'functioning' group. The synthesis score is yet further confirmation of adequate social functioning because the 10 points differential between positive and synthesis scores fall between the acceptable range differential, and the figure 84 (the totality of certain and uncertain answers) on the positive index shows only four points' differential.

*This man functions adequately in society without needing help or support.*

## Comment on relationship between score totals

Positive index score of 72/84 shows a 12-point swing between definite and uncertain answers. To seventeen questions he gave answers in terms of satisfaction and to six questions he gave 'perhaps' or uncertain answers. This too is within normal limits. However one must note that, although functioning well, he carries some uncertainties (perhaps insecurities) although this does not seem to be a handicap to him (perhaps even the opposite, i.e. potential?). The negative index score (8/26) carries only two certain answers and thirteen uncertain answers. This man is more certain about his satisfactions than about his frustrations: why? As he allows uncertain as well as certain answers to appear on his score, this indicates a lack of rigidity. He says in fact: 'I am sure about many aspects of my life but I have many doubts too.'

If one takes the low positive response (added up from his 'yes' or certain answers) and compares this with the aggregate negative score (i.e. added up from his certain and uncertain answers) this gives one 72/26. If one then takes the worst situation that this man is reporting, one finds that at the 'lowest' functioning level he still scores within normal healthy range, but his frustrations are then over one-third by comparison. If one takes the aggregate positive, comparing this with

the low negative (i.e. 84/8), there seems to appear a very
satisfactory perception of living. (As he probably moves
within these two ranges of self-perception one might ask: is
his high frustration in fact the result of his low perception,
when his heightened experience of frustration may move him
into action, which eventually will be felt as satisfying?)

The comparison of the positive index with that of the synthesis index, taking into consideration what has been said
above, shows *a man with excellent functioning at the time
when the scale was administered to him.*

## Comment on the internal consistencies and inconsistencies of the positive index

*Work* (full-time earner)
*Score-pattern: a:4:b:4:c:4:d:0:e:4:* (16/16)
Work is very satisfactory to this man in every respect. (Is he
in fact so much satisfied that he does not need an outside
interest? Is work really his field of interest?)

*Financial* (full-time earner)
*Score-pattern: a:4:b:4:c:4:d:4:e:2:* (16/18)
There is little problem in being financially satisfied, but why
is this man *feeling* financially not quite secure? (Is his uncertainty in fact due to some other insecurity? It must be so,
because all his other responses are positive.)

*Friendship*
*Score-pattern: a:4:b:2:c:2:d:4:e:4:* (12/16)
Although he reports having a close friend in whom he can
confide, he is uncertain whether people outside his family
really care about him. (Do we pick up here, for the second
time, his feeling of insecurity?) He says, in fact, that he is open
to others, but unsure of others' relationship to him. He has
reservations about making acquaintances. (If he is uncertain
whether people do care about him, can he really confide in a
close friend?)

*Primary family* (This section had been scored, but not added
to the total positive score. In the case of married people,

the secondary family is added up.)
*Score-pattern: a:4:b:4:c:4:d:4:e:4:* (20/20)
He perceives the past as entirely satisfactory. (Whence does
his insecurity come? Does it lie, perhaps, between the periods
of childhood and the present?)

*Secondary family* (spouse and children if married or cohabi-
ting)
*Score-pattern: a:2:b:4:c:4:d:4:e:4:* (16/18)
The marriage is reported to be satisfactory, yet he is uncertain about his interest in his wife's activities. (Are her
interests 'feminine'? Is he so absorbed in himself that he
does not take much notice of her interests? But he is honest
enough to say so. Does his partial lack of interest bother
his wife?)

*Personal*
*Score-pattern: a:4:b:4:c:4:d:2:e:2:* (12/16)
This man confirms in this section his satisfaction with his
marriage and sexual life. He is once more uncertain about his
liking to be with children. (Does this refer to his adolescent
son only, or children in particular? In the light of his own
high childhood satisfaction scores, why is this so?) He is also
unsure about his ability to be able to relax. (Do we pick up
now definitely a feeling of insecurity, though not specified?)

*Summary of positive index* This man reports high satisfaction
with his present life, although he has some feelings of insecurity colouring this picture. (Is there a slight tendency to
be somewhat egotistic?)

**Comment on the internal consistencies and inconsistencies
of the negative index**

*(Paralysis of) activity*
*Score-pattern: a:2:b:0:c:0:d:0:e:0:* (0/2)
The only section where some uncertain response is being
reported is his feeling of being overworked. In the light of
his other responses, this must relate to his perception of
reality.

*Somatic*
*Score-pattern: a:0:b:2:c:0:d:2:e:2:* (0/6)
This area carries some degree of uncertainty. (Is it possible
that his other insecurities may stem from here?) Why is his
imagination *perhaps* (or at times) being felt as painful? (He
is an artist. Does this relate to his work, or to some aspects
of his life outside work? Or both?)

*Persecution*
*Score-pattern: a:0:b:0:c:0:d:0:e:4:* (4/4)
He does not report any feeling of persecution. One answer
that stands out is his wish for more power and influence. As
he had reported in the positive index high work satisfaction
and adequate opportunity for getting ahead in his work, does
this frustration (which is so definitely stated among so many
'uncertain' scores in the scale so far) refer to his not-yet-
achieved ambitions? (or to his wish to improve in many ways
the content of his work?)

*Depression*
*Score-pattern: a:0:b:2:c:2:d:0:e:2:* (0/6)
Although not very depressed, he is aware of some insecurity
and some feeling of guilt. (Why the guilt?) His uncertain
answer to the question: 'Do you often find that people are
unappreciative of your effort?' may explain (or does it?) his
wish to have more power and influence. Does this response
refer to his private life (remembering that he felt that,
outside the family, people may not care for him) or to his
work? (Is his work accepted by those whom he may hold in
high regard? It may also refer to high libido-drives.) Once
more: why the guilt?

*Escape-routes*
*Score-pattern: a:0:b:2:c:2:d:4:e:0:* (4/8)
In the positive index this man reported his uncertainty
about his ability to be able to relax. Here he reports that
'perhaps' or 'occasionally' he is taking medicine to help him
to relax. He also 'perhaps' or 'at times' feels over-active, and
over-excited. (He had reported in the Activity section that he
feels he is perhaps overworked.) His only other definite reply

in the negative index is in relation to eating too much (he had underlined that this is what he was referring to). Insecurity and some anxiety manifests itself.

*Summary of negative index* The pattern of uncertainty and insecurity manifests in this index too. There appears some concern about health (which may perhaps cause this feeling). He states some feeling of guilt and a wish for more power and influence.

## Comparison of consistencies and inconsistencies between positive, negative and synthesis indexes

The analysis of the synthesis index confirms that this man's 'feeling tone' about his achieved ambition is 16 (out of 20), and in consequence this would explain his wish for more power and influence. (What does the word 'ambition' really mean to him? Is it in the area of work?) In the light of his ambitions, why does he score 18 points about his hope for the future? (Anxiety again? Perhaps connected with health?) It seems that it is in the area of meaning (17) that further fulfilment may be sought after, because life has, after all, given this man full opportunity (20) for self-expression. There is something in the past too (17) that raises doubt as to whether it was worth the struggle. (Something then had happened between childhood and adulthood which causes anxiety and doubt, and perhaps guilt too.)

He reported full satisfaction with work (with the exception of *interest*); full satisfaction in the financial area, except some uncertainty of *feeling* financially secure; full satisfaction with his family of origin; full satisfaction with his marriage, except the ability to relax and to be with children, and also some uncertainty as to whether he fully shared his wife's interests. On the basis of this there are the following possibilities (deduced from his scale responses) as to what 'ambition', not yet fulfilled, might mean to him:

1) area of interest (on the synthesis, meaning is 17): this could be a reaching out for something beyond work (seeking to liberate himself from the negative aspects of the unconscious);

2) establishing financial security on the feeling level too;
3) extending himself to others: wife, children, friends;
4) the ability to relax without resort to drug or medicine.

## Summary of scale interpretation

This is the profile of a forty-four-year-old man who functions well in society and is able to use his frustrations creatively, and yet he is not fulfilled as *he* wishes to be. (Something between childhood and adulthood keeps him uncertain about many aspects of his life, and he has not yet achieved his ambition, which probably means a need to grow further emotionally or spiritually. He needs to extend himself towards others, in which case he could use his full potential.)

## Brief notes about the above case

The interpreter of this case had only the scale responses available to him. Before sharing it, the patient was asked to write down briefly his life-situation and his problems as he saw them at about the time when his scale was recorded. (This scale was self-administered as part of an experiment. The patient was *asked* to fill in his replies; he did not seek help.) The letter, extracts from which appear below, was seen by the interpreter only *after* he had given his interpretation.

I have achieved some distinction in my field; I am quite well known I suppose. I love my wife, my son, but he at times irritates me. When I am struggling with my darkroom work I resent being disturbed. After a very happy childhood in Slovakia, I too (I know that you had been persecuted by the Nazis too) had been deported to various camps. However hard I am trying, I still suspect people. It is getting better as the years go by. At a particular camp in Germany, I became in charge of a group of prisoners in a stone quarry. I tried to remain human, under inhuman conditions, but still a great many prisoners died under my charge. I wasn't of course directly responsible, yet I feel that I share some responsibility . . . .

I love my wife, but the activities of the Ladies' Guild leave me somewhat cold. I lost God in the camps. Was it you, who wrote (I think it was Elie Wiesel) that God was crucified, with the crucifixion of some

British POWs in Buchenwald? I cannot believe. I wish I could .... '

The following scale was administered in Vancouver, Canada, and interpreted in California and London by two trained interpreters who were given only the scale's face sheet as reproduced below.

| | SCALE | TOTALS<br>T(4s)/T(4+2s) | MEAN<br>TOTAL |
|---|---|---|---|
| Age 34, two children | SCALE | | |
| (boy, girl, in teens) | POSITIVE | 48/52 | 50 |
| Nurse, female, | NEGATIVE | 48/56 | 52 |
| separated, white; | SYNTHESIS | – | 54 |

| POSITIVE SCALE | | | | | | | | NEGATIVE SCALE | | | | | | | SYNTHESIS | |
|---|---|---|---|---|---|---|---|---|---|---|---|---|---|---|---|---|
| Area | Part | 1 | 2 | 3 | 4 | 5 | Totals | Area | 1 | 2 | 3 | 4 | 5 | Totals | | |
| | A | 4 | 4 | 4 | 4 | 0 | | activity | 0 | 2 | 4 | 0 | 2 | 4/8 | 1) | 0 |
| work | B | 4 | 0 | 4 | 4 | 2 | 12/14 | somatic | 4 | 0 | 0 | 4 | 4 | 12/12 | 2) | 10 |
| | C | 0 | 0 | 4 | 4 | 4 | | persecution | 0 | 0 | 4 | 2 | 4 | 8/10 | 3) | 18 |
| finance | A | 0 | 0 | 0 | 0 | 0 | 0/0 | depression | 4 | 4 | 2 | 0 | 4 | 12/14 | 4) | 6 |
| friendship | | 4 | 4 | 4 | 4 | 4 | 20/20 | escape routes | 0 | 0 | 4 | 4 | 4 | 12/12 | 5) | 20 |
| family | A<br>B | 0 | 0 | 0 | 0 | 2 | 0/2 | | | | | Totals: | | 48/56 | | 54 |
| personal | B | 0 | 4 | 4 | 4 | 4 | 16/16 | | | | | | | | | |
| | | | | | | Totals: | 48/52 | | | | | | | | | |

## First interpretation

### General comment

Positive index of 48 places patient in range needing support. Negative mean of 52 indicates overwhelming frustration. Synthesis of 54 confirms positive mean of 50 (within 6-8 points) - answers are consistent. Positive swing of 4 points indicates somewhat inflexible. Negative swing of 8 points indicates more flexibility. There is more uncertainty in frustrations than in satisfactions. Criss-cross indicates at best frustration a little less than satisfaction (48-52 = 4 points), at worst overwhelming frustration (48 − 56 + 8 points). (Criss-cross refers to the lowest positive and highest negative totals in comparison, and the highest positive and lowest negative totals in comparison, i.e. 48-56; 52-48.) Need for help confirmed by all indexes.

*Positive scale*

*Work* Patient performs three roles: employed person, housewife and unemployed person. Main role is housewife. (I presume she is temporarily unemployed.) Patient scores highest as employed person, yet housewife is seen as main role. Probable conflict in roles. As employed person, high satisfaction except that she does not have enough opportunity for getting ahead. (What does this mean?) As housewife, she lacks social contacts and is uncertain about remaining a housewife. Again, is this conflict? As an unemployed person she wants to get back to work. In short, a woman playing two roles, but getting a lot of satisfaction out of work. (I conclude her satisfaction will increase as soon as she gets back to work.)

*Finance* Zero score. No satisfaction. Suggests a financial crisis.

*Friendship* Complete satisfaction. Probable flooding [too much going into one area at the expense of other areas]. When compared with finance, presents a black-and-white picture or compartmentalization of problems. In comparing work, finance and friendship, patient presents a very clear picture to herself of what is wrong - money and need for a job. She says: 'don't ask me about anything else'. The perhaps answer in work now seems very significant. Is she covering up something?

*Family A* A very black area. Uncertainty in family turning to her with their problems. Does she still want something from them? The perhaps answer likely quite significant. Again, an all-or-nothing picture for the area.

*Personal B* High score. Does not enjoy being single. (I have a hunch that this answer (being single) may be related to the doubt about being content to remain a housewife and the zero score on finances.) Does she mean, if I had a husband I could be a housewife and I would have no money problems? Again, a very simple pattern of solutions to a problem. What went wrong in the marriage?

*Negative scale*

*Activity* Her mind is underactive. Is this related to her unemployed status? Uncertainty in being too tired to work is not in keeping with being unemployed. Possible indication of depression. Uncertainty in being frustrated from doing things properly - what frustrates her, people or things? Is this her situation?

*Somatic* Headaches, concern about health and painful imagination point to tendency to somatize frustration?

*Persecution* Circumstances are the problem; perhaps people are against her. She clearly wants more power and influence. Likely power to do things; not a usual answer with women.

*Depression* Fairly high score. Depression, insecurity and people unappreciative of her efforts. Perhaps guilty. Here she says, 'I do a lot, I'm active, but people do not appreciate me.' Does this mean her concept of relationships is one of doing? Here is the first clear indication of a problem with people.

*Escape-routes* Over-activity or over-excitement, food and an extensive use of escape-routes. Over-activity confirms her as an active person, a 'doer'. Trouble with people confirms difficulty in relationships. (Now I have a picture of a 'driven' woman.)

*Synthesis*

Zero on ambition is a very depressed score. Contrasts with satisfaction in work role. Seems inconsistent.

Ten on future also suggests depression. She's not sure of a way out. (Is this related to her single status and a sense of difficulty with people?)

Eighteen on meaning likely relates to housewife role, friendship and personal areas.

Six on self-expression confirms zero on ambition.

Twenty on struggle supports eighteen on meaning.

Synthesis scores confirm a pattern of putting problems into certain areas.

*Summary*

A depressed woman, experiencing a great deal of frustration, who compartmentalizes her problem and puts a solution into work and possibly a husband. She does not look at areas related to people, but gives clues that all is not well.

She puts the blame on circumstances and sees the situation in terms of more assertion. She suffers considerably (tiredness, somatic complaints, escape-routes) from her frustration and is unable to use it constructively. Her strength is her acknowledgement of her frustration.

Likely a dependent person who copes with life through activity. Needs concrete help in work and finance areas. (What is her ambition?)

### Second interpretation

*General comment*

This woman falls into the 'at risk' band and has a very small swing in her score, indicating a somewhat rigid thinking. The negative scale is very high and overwhelms the positive, thus leaving her very considerably at risk.

*Positive scale:*

*Work* Scored as a worker; life is satisfactory, but her work has little future for her. As a housewife she scores slightly lower. The domestic satisfactions are offset by a lack of social life and the feeling she would like to do something else. Scored as an unemployed person, she is even less satisfied.

*Financial* This area shows very considerable stress. (This may be a reality situation in view of the separated woman's difficulty in raising a family on her own, but the problem about spending suggests more personal anxiety.)

*Friendship* This apparently satisfactory score shows a high reliance on the support of friends but may prove on examination to be somewhat unreal.

*Family* This near-nil score shows a deeply insecure and un-happy childhood which is felt by this woman to have been disabling. She is doubtful if she would even want her family to turn to her with their problems.

*Personal* This is a relatively high score, showing that she gets satisfaction from the company of men and children and enjoys sex and says she can relax. She is unhappy in her separated state and in view of the anxieties already shown in the previous areas, it is doubtful that she can, in fact, relax.

### Negative scale

*Activity* There are frustrations in working. She finds herself tired, her mind is under-active and she feels frustrated. This would indicate the possibility of some depression.

*Somatic* The frustrations express themselves fairly strongly in this area, where she has headaches and concern about her health and painful fantasies.

*Persecution* She feels that circumstances, and occasionally people, are against her and wishes for enough power to break out of the net of frustration. There are indications here that she is happier in a somewhat masculine role.

*Depression* This area carries the highest frustration score. She feels very depressed, insecure, guilty and unappreciated. The guilt will relate to the painful fantasies referred to in the somatic area. The depression here confirms the frustration in the activity area.

*Escape-routes* Again a fairly high score. Frustration drives her into a tense over-activity and either under- or over-eating and actions which at times will cause trouble to herself or others.

### Synthesis

There is massive frustration in the area of ambition. This

may relate to achievement as wife and mother or it may relate much more to work. The overall picture suggests that this is a woman who functions best in a job situation and becomes frustrated when at home too long. Her score also indicates a sense of frustration in regard to self-expression, and here her answer in regard to hope for the future is reasonable. The two answers that seem highly inconsistent are the answers to question 3 in regard to 'meaningfulness' and to question 5 in regard to life being 'worth the struggle'.

## Summary

This is a young woman who, at this point of time, is deeply frustrated in her life situation. Her separated state causes her much unhappiness but there are indications that she has problems in relation to men. There would appear to be considerable reality problems but these are made more difficult by her own fantasies. The early deprivations colour her feeling about life and make her feel that circumstances are against her. She needs very much to be contained in her work situation which will give her enough scope and she needs help in greater self-understanding.

## Measuring improvement

The following three scales show a pattern of change over time.

Female age 34
divorced 3 children
(girls 16, 13, 11)

| SCALE | TOTALS T(4s)/T(4+2s) | MEAN TOTAL | First test February 1969 |
|---|---|---|---|
| POSITIVE | 40/44 | 42 | |
| NEGATIVE | 52/54 | 53 | |
| SYNTHESIS | – | 42 | |

**POSITIVE SCALE**

| Area | Part | 1 | 2 | 3 | 4 | 5 | Totals |
|---|---|---|---|---|---|---|---|
| work | B | 4 | 4 | 2 | 0 | 0 | 8/10 |
| | D | 4 | 4 | 2 | 0 | 2 | |
| finance | B | 0 | 0 | 0 | 4 | 0 | 4/4 |
| friendship | | 4 | 4 | 4 | 2 | 4 | 16/18 |
| family | A | 0 | 0 | 0 | 0 | 0 | 0/0 |
| | B | 4 | 0 | 4 | 0 | 0 | |
| personal | B | 4 | 4 | 4 | 0 | 0 | 12/12 |
| | | | | | | Totals: | 40/44 |

**NEGATIVE SCALE**

| Area | 1 | 2 | 3 | 4 | 5 | Totals |
|---|---|---|---|---|---|---|
| activity | 4 | 0 | 0 | 4 | 4 | 12/12 |
| somatic | 0 | 4 | 0 | 0 | 0 | 4/4 |
| persecution | 4 | 0 | 4 | 0 | 4 | 12/12 |
| depression | 4 | 4 | 4 | 0 | 0 | 12/12 |
| escape routes | 4 | 0 | 4 | 4 | 2 | 12/14 |
| | | | | | Totals: | 52/54 |

**SYNTHESIS**

| | |
|---|---|
| 1) | 1 |
| 2) | 10 |
| 3) | 10 |
| 4) | 1 |
| 5) | 20 |
| | 42 |

Female age 34
divorced 3 children
(girls 16, 13, 11)

| | SCALE | TOTALS<br>T(4s)/T(4+2s) | MEAN<br>TOTAL | Retest July 1969 |
|---|---|---|---|---|
| | POSITIVE | 60/62 | 61 | |
| | NEGATIVE | 12/14 | 13 | |
| | SYNTHESIS | – | 96 | |

| | POSITIVE SCALE | | | | | | | NEGATIVE SCALE | | | | | | | SYNTHESIS |
|---|---|---|---|---|---|---|---|---|---|---|---|---|---|---|---|
| Area | Part | 1 | 2 | 3 | 4 | 5 | Totals | Area | 1 | 2 | 3 | 4 | 5 | Totals | |
| work | B | 4 | 4 | 0 | 4 | 0 | / | activity | 0 | 0 | 0 | 0 | 0 | 0/0 | 1) 18 |
| | D | 4 | 4 | 0 | 4 | 4 | 16/16 | somatic | 0 | 0 | 0 | 0 | 0 | 0/0 | 2) 20 |
| finance | C | 0 | 0 | 2 | 4 | 4 | 8/10 | personal | 2 | 0 | 0 | 0 | 4 | 4/6 | 3) 20 |
| friendship | | 4 | 4 | 4 | 4 | 4 | 20/20 | depression | 0 | 4 | 0 | 0 | 0 | 4/4 | 4) 18 |
| family | A | 0 | 0 | 4 | 0 | 0 | 4/4 | escape routes | 0 | 0 | 0 | 4 | 0 | 4/4 | 5) 20 |
| | B | | | | | | | | | | Totals: | | | 12/14 | 96 |
| personal | B | 0 | 4 | 4 | 0 | 4 | 12/12 | | | | | | | | |
| | | | | | Totals: | | 60/62 | | | | | | | | |

Female age 34
divorced 3 children
(girls 16, 13, 11)

| | SCALE | TOTALS<br>T(4s)/T(4+2s) | MEAN<br>TOTAL | Third test June 1970 |
|---|---|---|---|---|
| | POSITIVE | 76/80 | 78 | |
| | NEGATIVE | 8/10 | 9 | |
| | SYNTHESIS | – | 94 | |

| | POSITIVE SCALE | | | | | | | NEGATIVE SCALE | | | | | | | SYNTHESIS |
|---|---|---|---|---|---|---|---|---|---|---|---|---|---|---|---|
| Area | Part | 1 | 2 | 3 | 4 | 5 | Totals | Area | 1 | 2 | 3 | 4 | 5 | Totals | |
| work | B | 4 | 4 | 0 | 4 | 0 | / | activity | 0 | 0 | 0 | 0 | 0 | 0/0 | 1) 15 |
| | D | 4 | 4 | 0 | 4 | 4 | 16/16 | somatic | 0 | 0 | 0 | 0 | 0 | 0/0 | 2) 19 |
| finance | C | 4 | 0 | 4 | 4 | 2 | 12/14 | personal | 0 | 0 | 0 | 0 | 2 | 0/2 | 3) 20 |
| friendship | | 4 | 4 | 4 | 4 | 4 | 20/20 | depression | 0 | 4 | 0 | 0 | 0 | 4/4 | 4) 20 |
| family | A | 2 | 4 | 4 | 0 | 4 | 12/14 | escape routes | 0 | 0 | 0 | 4 | 0 | 4/4 | 5) 20 |
| | B | | | | | | / | | | | Totals: | | | 8/10 | 94 |
| personal | B | 0 | 4 | 4 | 4 | 4 | 16/16 | | | | | | | | |
| | | | | | Totals: | | 76/80 | | | | | | | | |

## Decision-making

On the basis of the scale reproduced overleaf, priority had been given to the treatment of this patient: immediate counselling was offered.

Female age 53
divorced no children
completed grade school
Retired - nursery work
$1,000-1,499
white

| SCALE | TOTALS T(4s)/T(4+2s) | MEAN TOTAL |
|---|---|---|
| POSITIVE | 32/36 | 34 |
| NEGATIVE | 72/72 | 72 |
| SYNTHESIS | – | 42 |

A.N.D. – Nursing Home

**POSITIVE SCALE**

| Area | Part | 1 | 2 | 3 | 4 | 5 | Totals |
|---|---|---|---|---|---|---|---|
| work | E | 0 | 2 | 0 | 4 | 0 | 4/6 |
| finance | A | 0 | 4 | 0 | 0 | 0 | 4/4 |
| friendship | | 0 | 0 | 2 | 0 | 4 | 4/6 |
| family | A | 0 | 0 | 0 | 0 | 4 | 4/4 |
| | B | | | | | | |
| personal | B | 0 | 4 | 4 | 4 | 4 | 16/16 |
| | | | | Totals: | | | 32/36 |

**NEGATIVE SCALE**

| Area | 1 | 2 | 3 | 4 | 5 | Totals |
|---|---|---|---|---|---|---|
| activity | 0 | 4 | 0 | 4 | 4 | 12/12 |
| somatic | 0 | 4 | 0 | 4 | 4 | 12/12 |
| personal | 4 | 0 | 4 | 4 | 0 | 12/12 |
| depression | 4 | 4 | 4 | 4 | 4 | 20/20 |
| escape routes | 0 | 4 | 4 | 4 | 4 | 16/16 |
| | | | | Totals: | | 72/72 |

**SYNTHESIS**

| | |
|---|---|
| 1) | 4 |
| 2) | 1 |
| 3) | 5 |
| 4) | 17 |
| 5) | 15 |
| | 42 |

Medical diagnosis

1) chronic obstructive lung disease with large asthmatic component
2) congestive heart failure
3) depressive neuroses
   Attempted suicide

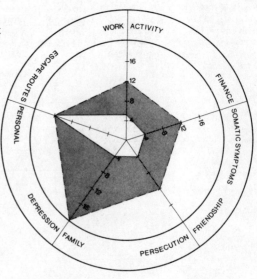

It can be seen from the diagram that frustrations here are overwhelming satisfactions. The straight lines indicate the perimeter of the satisfaction area; the shaded area frustration.

## Indication of danger

This patient was found dead within four days of administration of the scale. One of the advantages of using the scale is to be able to prevent possible suicide.

Female age 46
separated two children
(male, 25, female, 26)
some high school
housewife (machinist)
white

| SCALE | TOTALS T(4s)/T(4+2s) | MEAN TOTAL |
|---|---|---|
| POSITIVE | 48/56 | 52 |
| NEGATIVE | 64/72 | 68 |
| SYNTHESIS | – | 37 |

**POSITIVE SCALE**

| Area | Part | 1 | 2 | 3 | 4 | 5 | Totals |
|---|---|---|---|---|---|---|---|
| work | B | 4 | 2 | 0 | 4 | 4 | 12/14 |
| | C | 0 | 0 | 2 | 4 | 4 | |
| finance | B | 0 | 4 | 0 | 4 | 0 | 8/8 |
| friendship | | 4 | 0 | 2 | 4 | 4 | 12/14 |
| family | A | 0 | 2 | 0 | 0 | 4 | |
| | B | 2 | 4 | 4 | 0 | 0 | 8/10 |
| personal | A | 0 | 0 | 2 | 4 | 4 | 8/10 |
| | | | | | | Totals: | 48/56 |

**NEGATIVE SCALE**

| Area | 1 | 2 | 3 | 4 | 5 | Totals |
|---|---|---|---|---|---|---|
| activity | 0 | 2 | 2 | 0 | 4 | 4/8 |
| somatic | 4 | 4 | 0 | 0 | 0 | 8/8 |
| personal | 4 | 4 | 4 | 4 | 4 | 20/20 |
| depression | 4 | 4 | 4 | 4 | 4 | 20/20 |
| escape routes | 2 | 4 | 4 | 2 | 4 | 12/16 |
| | | | | | Totals: | 64/72 |

**SYNTHESIS**

1) 1
2) 2
3) 20
4) 13
5) 1

37

# Appendix: Effectiveness of the Scale in Treatment

The effect of the scale in treatment has been described by a social worker to whom, as part of her training, the scale was administered. As this is typical of many of the answers received, her comments are reproduced here.

During the first interview I found a great relief in expressing my problems, frustrations and satisfactions - a catharsis.

I expressed nothing I hadn't said to myself many times before; however, somehow the picture seemed clearer, less complicated, and therefore I seemed to view things with less pessimism.

I answered all questions with thought. However, I found I could answer some with no hesitation and others with more difficulty. At that time I did not really have enough time to wonder why.

Since the initial interview a particular situation will bring a question to mind and I will attempt to determine why I answered the way that I did, or why I hesitated and/or why I would answer differently now.

In trying to understand why I answered the question the way I did I gain a good deal of insight into that particular area, why I'm responding the way I am, what messages I'm giving people, my family, and why they are responding the way they do to these messages.

While giving the results of the questionnaire I remembered that the interviewer said that it indicated I was satisfied with my work and not so satisfied in the family, possibly in my marriage. I was surprised but in thinking about this it seemed true.

In answering 'Do you want more power and influence?' I had said 'yes' or 'perhaps'. The interviewer suggested that since I was satisfied with my work the power and influence desired was probably in relationship to my marriage. This now seemed so clear. There was the conflict. I had purposely married a domineering man, yet since the marriage I was struggling to dominate. I decided I'd better make up my mind what I really wanted.

No really big change came about until a number of weeks later when I was listening to a summary in connection with a patient. The consultant said something about 'Had this woman ever wanted to be a wife to her husband?'

This prompted a great deal of thought about my role as a wife. In addition, although I had answered 'no' to the question, 'Is sex an unwelcomed activity in your life?' I had been more aware that I had been turning away from my husband's sexual overtures. (The only way I could have power and influence?)

I decided not to do this any longer. I would be responsive to him. This change in my attitude has had its effects on him and on me in other areas of our relationship. I feel we had a fairly good relationship before the Heimler test. It's just that much better. It's been like giving up an unnecessary struggle. I have felt a closeness I've not felt in a number of years. For instance, he is discussing his business, business activities, and plans (something he has been reluctant to do in the past) and in turn he is less likely to turn a deaf ear when I discuss work. There has been an opening up of communication in areas lacking in communication for a number of years (money), and I have a more positive feeling about the future, as if this is only the beginning.

As a *diagnostic instrument* the scale offers several items of information.*

1) (a)  It indicates the patient's *level* of functioning and consequently the need for service.
   (b)  It indicates the degree of 'risk' or 'crisis', helping the worker or therapist to recognize which patients need immediate service.
   (c)  It provides a *picture* of the patient's functioning.
   (d)  It provides measures of behaviour, e.g. anxiety, rigidity, denial.
   (e)  It identifies problem areas.
2) The scale and the written interpretation provide material for the case record and may provide an alternative for the 'social history'.
3) The scale provides uniform communication between therapists and social workers, between social workers and supervisors, and between agencies; also between all those who have been trained in the interpretation of the scale.

---

* Peter H. Taylor, 'Report on the Heimler Project', Santa Clara County Welfare Department unpublished report (California 1970).

4) The scale can be used to measure change effected in the patient by administration of the scale over a period of time.

# Index

work, 20
    patients' experience of, 47-8
    useless, effects of, 5
    *see also* case studies 2, 6; un-
    employment